An Angel
Healed Me

An Angel Healed Me

True Stories of Heavenly Encounters

Theresa Cheung

POCKET
BOOKS

LONDON • SYDNEY • NEW YORK • TORONTO

First published in Great Britain in 2010 by Simon & Schuster UK Ltd
A CBS COMPANY

Copyright © 2010 by Theresa Cheung

3 5 7 9 10 8 6 4 2

Simon & Schuster UK Ltd
1st Floor
222 Gray's Inn Road
London
WC1X 8HB

www.simonandschuster.co.uk

Simon & Schuster Australia
Sydney

A CIP catalogue copy for this book
is available from the British Library.

ISBN: 978-1-84983-010-2

Typeset in Bembo by M Rules
Printed by CPI Cox & Wyman, Reading, Berkshire RG1 8EX

Contents

Acknowledgements

So many people helped create this book that it is hard to know where to start. Words cannot express how much I am indebted to my agent, Clare Hulton, for believing in and making this book happen, to my editor, Kerri Sharp, for her vision and encouragement, and to my copyeditor, Monica O'Connell, and everyone at Simon and Schuster for being so very helpful throughout the entire process of writing this book and getting it ready for publication.

I'd also like to take this opportunity to sincerely thank everyone who was generous enough to share their incredible stories, experiences and personal thoughts with me along the way and for allowing me to use them here. I'm deeply grateful to you all because you are the heart and spirit of this book and I have no doubt that your stories will bring hope and healing to many.

Special thanks to Ray, Robert and Ruthie for their love and patience while I went into exile to complete this project. And last, but by no means least, special thanks to everyone who reads this book. May it open your eyes and your heart to the wonder that exists within and around you.

'You Are Never Alone'

You are never alone . . .
Your guardian angel is right beside you
Always ready to help,
At the slightest need . . .
But first, you must believe . . .

Author unknown

Introduction:
Called by an Angel

We've never had to look far to find our angels.
Angels have never really been out of reach. We
can always discover angels from the inside-out,
because it is the angel inside us who can point
the way to all our other angels.

Author unknown

Twenty-five years spent studying, researching and writing about
the paranormal has taught me a lot of things. I know that life is
a mystery and that things occur in this world for which there are
no lasting explanations. I understand that an open mind may be
the greatest virtue. I have also come to believe, without any
doubt, that there are healing angels in our midst.

I believe that loved ones watch over us from the other side and
that each one of us has a guardian angel who walks with us
through the journey of our lives. I believe that our guardian angels
can manifest their healing presence in countless different ways. In
rare instances they may appear in their full-blown glory, complete
with wings and halo, but more often than not they will appear in

subtler, gentler ways: as a feather, a cloud, a gentle breeze, a compelling dream, a hug, a song, a mysterious scent, a vision, a flicker of light, an amazing coincidence, a flash of insight or an unseen yet very real presence that somehow instructs, comforts and protects us. They may also choose to manifest through other people who are consciously or unconsciously guided by those from a spiritual dimension. Last, but by no means least, they may appear or express themselves through the spirits of departed loved ones.

During the many years I've been gathering collections of real-life angel stories from people of all ages and backgrounds, I've discovered that even though all the stories are unique they all have one overriding theme in common and that is the theme of healing, whether that healing be physical, emotional or spiritual. I have also noticed that each angel story in itself can be a messenger of healing. This is because whenever moving and life-affirming stories are shared they work their healing magic on those who read or hear them, even if these people have not had an angel experience themselves, by reminding them that forces for love and goodness are at work in the world and that miracles really can, and do, happen.

Looking back I can see that almost from the very beginning this 'healing angel' theme was always there in the background, calling out to me, waiting for me to wake up, acknowledge and embrace it.

A wake-up call

About twelve or so years ago my health took a turn for the worse and I just couldn't understand why. I felt as if I was falling apart.

I was anxious and moody; it was difficult to concentrate. I was depressed one moment, agitated the next, perpetually tired and had mood swings like Jekyll and Hyde. Some days even walking up the stairs made me feel like crying. I was in my early thirties but I felt like I was in my late nineties.

After several months of feeling terrible I went to see my doctor, hoping for a cure; but this was to be the first of many visits. My doctor couldn't figure out what was wrong with me beyond the sense of *Who isn't tired nowadays?* Each time I saw him he told me to relax, get some rest and come back in a few months. And each time I did try to relax, but my health seemed to deteriorate even further. My husband was worried about me. I was worried about me. To make matters worse we'd been trying for a baby for more than a year with no success.

It took several years for me to finally be diagnosed with polycystic ovary syndrome, or PCOS, and to discover that the symptoms of this condition were making me feel tired and limiting my chances of getting pregnant. In the mid- to late 1990s there just wasn't as much available information about polycystic ovaries as there is today, and I can still remember vividly the shot to my heart when an uninformed ultrasound technician told me that I might never be able to have children. When I went back to my doctor for advice and support he admitted that he knew very little about the condition and referred me to a gynaecologist who might be able to help. It took nearly five months for me to get that appointment and then many more months for me to receive proper advice and treatment. Looking back, those long and uncertain months were perhaps both the worst and the best of my life.

At the time, many of my friends were having kids and asking me when I was going to have them. This hadn't bothered me before: I thought we had all the time in the world to have kids. After my diagnosis, though, those words from the ultrasound technician really scared me. I'd never been that maternal but I'd always thought I'd be able to have kids one day. Now that day might never come. I wasn't sure if I could cope. I felt more insecure about myself than I had ever done. Some days I didn't even want to be around people. I felt a failure as a wife and as a woman because my body couldn't do what came naturally to other women. I felt like I was losing myself piece by piece every day. Even talking on the phone to friends became an ordeal. I had to pretend that everything would be okay, that I was fine, when in reality I was tearing myself up inside.

After several months of uncertainty and confusion I started to think I was losing my mind. I couldn't find the strength that I had relied on for so many other low points in my life. Trying and failing to get pregnant and feeling constantly exhausted and unattractive because I was gaining weight and breaking out in spots (I didn't know at the time that these are also common symptoms of polycystic ovaries) brought my faith in angels to an all-time low. I didn't know if angels existed or not and I didn't seem to care. All this wasn't making me a stronger or more loving person. It did quite the opposite. I was a nightmare to be around.

Above all, though, I was tired. Tired of hoping and of that

terrible feeling each month when another chance of getting pregnant vanished. I didn't feel like me any more. I couldn't get past feelings of failure and loss. All I could think was, 'Why me?'

Friends told me to stay hopeful, as there was a lot that could be done for women who couldn't get pregnant naturally, but in my mind I had already given up. A part of me believed this was some kind of punishment for my lack of maternal instinct. I'd never been one of those women who long to hold babies – in fact I'd always steered well clear of them. Come to think of it, I'd never even held a baby and being around children made me feel uncomfortable. I wasn't natural. I clearly wasn't meant to be a mother. I didn't deserve children.

I wasn't just hurting for myself. I was hurting for my husband, a loving and kind man who adored children and I couldn't give them to him. Why had the angels given him a wife who couldn't do this? He tried to stay strong and tell me he knew it would happen one day but I didn't believe him. Not without major expensive medical miracles that we could not afford. We were not rich by any stretch. I often thought about leaving my husband so he would be able to try again with someone else.

One afternoon about a year after my diagnosis the no-baby blackness descended again. I had just had a course of fertility treatment and was once again in that two-week waiting period to see if the results were positive or negative. I'd been here so many times before I didn't have the energy or the will to raise my hopes. I remember curling up on the sofa and trying to fall asleep so I could shut everyone and everything out, but just as I was nodding off the phone rang. I felt too heavy and tired to pick it up and just let it ring. It didn't stop ringing. I put my head under my cushion, but the ringing wouldn't stop.

Eventually, I stumbled over to pick the phone up, cursing myself for not switching the answerphone on that morning. I was greeted by the irritatingly friendly voice of a woman who called herself Suzanne. She said she had been given my number by my doctor and she belonged to an infertility-support network in my area. I felt sleepy and really didn't want to speak to her, so I tried to hang up, but she was very insistent. She said she needed only a few minutes of my time and then she would vanish. She told me that she understood how difficult things must feel for me at the moment but that I needed to stay positive because stress and negative thinking could actually make it harder for me to conceive. She also said that she was sorry that I wasn't pregnant right now but there were many other ways to mother apart from the biological. Then she told me that if I could relax and focus less on the idea of a baby and more on the feelings of love that a baby inspires everything would work out fine, whether I got pregnant or not. In the past year or so, since I'd been trying to get pregnant, countless people had given me unwanted advice; so all I could think about was getting her off the phone. I pretended to take down the details of her support group, pretended I was listening and then hung up.

As soon as I put the phone down, I heard this ringing tone in my ear. It puzzled me. It was so sharp and clear. I sat down and rubbed my ears but it still wouldn't go away. It took a good few minutes to disappear and as soon as it did I felt some of the heaviness in my body and mind lift. It seemed like a bolt of electricity had gone through me. I can't explain why but I felt more positive than I had ever done.

In what I can only describe as one of those brilliant 'aha' moments, it suddenly became obvious to me that my feelings of self-hatred were limiting my chances of getting pregnant; I wasn't providing the soul of my future child with a welcome home. I had to find a way to conquer this, and I realized in that instant that the only way to do this was to think of a baby not so much as a right, but as a privilege. I had to understand that not having a child didn't make me a failure or an incomplete person. I had to understand that there was a child within me who needed as much nurturing and love as any biological child I might have.

I wanted to speak to Suzanne again, to apologize for being so short with her and to ask for details of the meeting she'd mentioned. I made a call-back request but the number was not listed. I called my doctor to get her number or the number of her support network. Much to my surprise my doctor told me that he had never heard of Suzanne or her network and that he would never have given out contact details of his patients without their permission. I searched online and in my local library and no record of the network existed; none of my friends or my family had heard of it either. To all intents and purposes Suzanne didn't exist.

To this day I don't know who Suzanne was or how she got my number or even if I dreamed up the whole phone conversation.

But looking back now I can see that she was a healing angel sent from heaven to guide and comfort me, because when I was at my lowest point her calm and wise words helped shift my perception in a miraculous way. The road I was heading down was a terribly dark and dangerous one and she quite literally gave me a wake-up call.

After that phone call I made the decision to not let my life and my future happiness revolve around whether or not I could have children, and as soon as I did so it was like a weight fell off my shoulders. I started to laugh again. I started to feel like me again. The relief was incredible.

When my pregnancy test came back negative two weeks later I wasn't nearly as upset or distressed as everyone had expected me to be, myself included. It wasn't easy leaving self-pity and self-absorption behind but slowly, day by day, I made tentative steps. I started first with practical things. I sorted out my diet by cutting out the junk food I had used as a source of comfort. I forced myself to go for at least thirty minutes' brisk walking a day. I spent more time with the people I loved. I offered my services as a volunteer reading assistant at my local school and discovered once again that Suzanne had been right – there were other ways to bring children into your life. I began to understand, really understand, that there are many ways to 'mother' besides the biological.

I didn't expect it, or even long for it, but my change of heart and mind did work a miracle. Three months later I could not believe my eyes when my pregnancy test was positive. Eight months later I gave birth to a beautiful baby boy and two years after that I was blessed again with a gorgeous baby girl. My children mean the world to me and always will, but facing the possibility of never being able to have them may have been the best thing to have happened to me. It helped me to understand that having children wasn't ever going to make me feel complete. I could have dozens of kids and still feel empty inside if I didn't believe in or love myself. It opened my mind to the idea that the angels hadn't forgotten me and that I might just be worthy of their love and healing. They were simply waiting for me to stop drowning in doubt and self-pity and open my eyes and my heart to their love and light.

When I think back now to my angel wake-up call I truly believe I encountered an intersection between earthly experience and a higher realm. It was a supernatural moment. Previously, although I thought I believed in angels, deep down I still doubted whether they believed in me, because I had never actually heard, seen or felt their presence for myself, but after my angel phone call – as I like to think of it – my confidence grew and the veil between this life and the next gradually started to lift. It would take me a few more years to fully comprehend the wonder of it all, and I freely admit that much of what I am writing now is with the benefit of hindsight. Nonetheless I now believe that the clear voice that spoke to me on the phone that day was that of my guardian angel. I went on to have many other incredible healing-angel experiences, some of which were quite literally life saving and some of which I will share in this book; a book that I feel honoured but also destined to write.

A passion for miracles

The idea of angels has intrigued and inspired me for as long as I can remember, and not just because I've never been able to forget the moment when Clarence got his wings in *It's a Wonderful Life*. I've always been in love with the idea because I was born into a family of psychics and spiritualists and from an early age I was encouraged by my mother, who saw and heard angels all her life, to believe in angels.

It's only in the last ten years, though, that I have really begun to understand that, while I couldn't see angels in the same way that my mother could, all along they were speaking to me through dreams, feelings and thoughts or the words or actions of other people, even if I didn't realize it at the time. For example, when I was pregnant with my son and driving my car towards a busy junction, did my departed mother whisper in my ear and urge me to turn right instead of left? Had I turned left, as I had fully intended to before an angel called my name, I would almost certainly have died in a terrible road accident. Was it the love and guidance of an angel that gave me the strength to pull through bouts of depression and darkness, in my teens and again later in my early thirties? Did an angel save my eight-month-old son from falling down a flight of stairs?

It was a lifetime of dreaming come true then when I was given the opportunity to write this book about angel healing. I'd already written several books about angels and the psychic world, some of which went on to become bestsellers, and both my agent and my publisher agreed that this was the perfect project for me.

Coming from a rigorous academic background I always prided myself on presenting the evidence for an afterlife in an objective way, but all that changed years ago when my mailbox started to bulge with miraculous stories of healing and transformation sent to me by people all over the world. Almost all of these contemporary accounts of angel experiences were so inspiring and positive that I felt compelled to collect them together in book form, and share them with a wider audience, along with some of my own experiences. I was losing my objectivity and very possibly the backing of the academic community that had nurtured my inquisitive mind, but I was gaining a sense of purpose.

The arrival of angels in my life a decade or so ago has been the miracle that has transformed it. I have fallen in love with the very idea of angels. They have energized my life and my writing because I know that the words I am writing are for everyone. It took a while for me to see the light; and, as you'll see later, I've stumbled a lot and been plagued with so many doubts and fears on the way, but I now understand that I was being led on to this path from the very beginning.

I was meant to study, yearn for, look for and listen to angels. When I first started to write about angels I was nervous about how my work would be received, but the reaction has been overwhelmingly positive. And, as soon as I started asking people if they had any angel stories, over and over again I heard, 'Yes, this is what happened to me,' or, 'I'd like to share my story, my experience of angels with you.' I didn't have to look far at all. The stories flew in my direction, and continue to do so every day, via email, or people I encounter at work, meet in bookshops or even when I visit the dentist, proving to me that angels are all around us and that in all corners of the globe ordinary people are being touched and healed by something or someone that is giving them incredible faith.

All of us at times, even those who seem to have it all, cannot escape feelings of emptiness, a longing for something more than the day-to-day reality of our lives. Sometimes this feeling is like yearning for a warm and comforting place we can call our home, a place where there is no fear, tears or loneliness and where there is only love. Our rational minds can't see this place, but our hearts can feel it and sense that it may have something to do with paradise, nirvana, heaven or whatever name we want to give it. As we continue our inner search for hope and peace, our spirits long to find a piece of this heaven on earth.

The good news is that more and more ordinary people from all over the world are finding their own glimpses of heaven – and, as this book will make crystal clear, miracles are far more common than most of us think they are.

Here to stay

I'm often asked what an angel is and my answer is always the same: angels represent all that is good. They are spiritual creatures and forces of light and they love us for who we are and want the best for us. Religion doesn't come into it because everyone, regardless of belief system as well as age, colour or creed, has the potential to connect with angels in their own unique way. Neither are angels a so-called New Age phenomenon or a fad.

They have been with us since the beginning of time – even longer – and they are here to stay.

There are some people who have the extraordinary ability to actually see angels or the spirits of those who have passed, but I must point out that this is very rare. I certainly don't have this ability. It is much more common – and my angel phone call eleven years ago falls into this category – to experience a flash of profound insight or inspiration that somehow changes everything for the better. Also common are meaningful dreams, amazing coincidences, subtle signs (such as the appearance of a white feather at significant times or moments), familiar scents or sounds or simple but unexpected feelings of warmth, comfort and support during times of crisis. And sometimes angels will appear in animals or children or in the unexpected kindness of strangers or the spirits of departed loved ones. The possibilities for goodness to manifest itself in this life and offer tantalizing glimpses of the next are endless.

Right now, at this moment in time, people all over the world seem to be awakening to the presence of angels, as I discovered first hand when I started writing about angels. I received letters and emails from people all over the world, all firm in their belief that angelic intervention on earth is not only possible but actually happens every day. The key word here is *belief.*

There will always be sceptics who say that angels exist only in a person's imagination. I used to try to convince these people in a rational way that angels are real. I would tell them that angel stories have been recorded since the dawn of time in almost every culture. I would point to the huge number of angel stories I have collected as 'evidence'. In a court of law a witness statement is taken as evidence. But it soon became clear to me that as long as a person's heart and mind is closed to belief in angels, there is nothing that I, or anyone else, can say to make any difference. It is all a matter of faith and to those who have faith in angels – because they are in tune with the message of healing love and hope that angels bring, or because their lives have been touched in some way by angels – no explanation is necessary. Nothing will ever have the power and the strength of their belief that angels walk among us.

As I write this book angels are indeed everywhere. They are making their presence felt in the world as never before. There are television programmes, internet sites, books, newsletters, magazines and angel memorabilia. Publishers are noticing that interest in angels is increasing in a major way. Perhaps this rising interest in the topic of angels is the real key to understanding the significance of the year 2012: maybe we will not see the end of the world but will instead see the dawn of a new era in which limiting concepts about angels will disappear. Today angels are finally allowing us to know them on their own terms. They are emerging from religious strongholds and breaking through into public consciousness and the homes and hearts of people all over the world.

The re-emergence of angels has never been more critical. Sadly, time has not always brought us wisdom and compassion and the modern world remains one of pain, injustice and suffering. There have been incredible advances but these haven't stopped things going terribly wrong with humanity. Images of emaciated children, polluted landscapes and a world bombarded with violence and terror are screened into our homes every day. We urgently need to know that there is love, hope and goodness in the world and that the forces of goodness are strong enough to defeat the sorrow, injustice and pain we see around us. Using the experiences of ordinary people as beacons of hope, angels are now emerging as our messengers of love and healing by reminding us that the goodness we have forgotten still exists. They are guiding us to a new beginning, a new dawn. They are making themselves known to us through the voices of ordinary people with extraordinary, easily recognizable stories to tell, because we are crying out for them. And, the more we listen to and trust and believe in them, the closer to earth the angels will fly, bringing with them their pure, unselfish and healing love.

About this book

Having been for many years now in the fortunate position of reading and collecting angel stories, it has become crystal clear to me that you don't need to be an angel whisperer, clairvoyant, psychic or medium to see or hear angels. All you need is an open mind and a trusting heart. It took me too many long years to realize this essential truth, and in Chapter One you'll see that in my early adult life I tried perhaps harder than most to be 'psychic'.

Being born into a family of psychics and spiritualists meant I desperately wanted to see spirits and angels like my mother, grandmother and brother could. But the harder I tried the less I could see and feel them and the more alone and disappointed I felt with myself, my psychic abilities and my life. I had no idea that the angels were close by me, and that fear and my obsession with whether or not I had the 'gift' were closing my eyes, my heart and my mind to them.

By sharing some of my psychic journey with you in the first chapter of this book, I hope you will see that anyone – whatever their age and background and however sceptical or self-doubting of their abilities – can open their heart and have their lives healed and transformed by angels. You'll see that I'm not an angel lady, celebrity psychic, medium or spiritual guru; I'm an ordinary forty-five-year-old mum with no remarkable psychic or healing powers. But amazing things have happened to me, and continue to happen, that I simply can't explain. This has led me to believe that each one of us is born with natural psychic ability and that, even though layers of self-doubt, fear and pessimism can shut down our connection with the invisible realm as we get older, we can all find ways to cut through those layers and reclaim the love of angels and the spiritual healing or sense of wholeness that is our birthright.

After this outlining of some of my own experiences, so that readers may get a sense of where I am coming from and who I am, the remaining chapters form the heart of this book because they contain true stories sent to me by people of all ages whose bodies, minds and spirits have been healed in some remarkable way by angels. Many of the stories took place during times of great physical or emotional illness while others concern the terminally ill and dying and experiences that happened specifically in a hospital – whether to a patient, a member of staff or a visitor.

You'll read about stunning recoveries or well-timed premonitions that even the doctors involved in a patient's treatment say can be explained only by the existence of a higher power. There are also stories of angels intervening in times of danger or angels simply working their magic and bringing their healing lightness into everyday life.

True stories

In addition to the themes of physical, emotional and spiritual healing, another common narrative thread is that all the stories in this book are true and based in fact, not fantasy. However, while the identification of the exact cause of the healing miracles described may interest scientists, it is not the inspiration of this book. The love and power of angels is boundless and perhaps it is best to consider angel healing as a blessed gift and as a mystery that should not be solved (in terms of how or why it happens) but that should simply be embraced with gratitude.

The stories you will read show just some of the countless invisible and visible ways in which angels whisper their healing to us. Some of these stories are bizarre and totally unexplainable. Some will inspire, comfort or move you to tears while others may confound or even stretch your capacity to believe, but to the best of my knowledge they are all true accounts. The people who gave me permission to share their experiences or edit and write them up are ordinary human beings with opinions, jobs, lives and families. Many of them were extremely relieved to share their experiences, sometimes for the first time. I have no reason to doubt their integrity. In some cases names, dates and places may have been changed to protect the identity of those concerned because the contents of the stories are just too personal, but I can assure you they are as real as people can be. And they all have stories which are precious and extraordinary and which they want to share with a wider audience to show others that angels are with us even if we can't always see them.

Some of the people who submitted their stories already had a deep faith in angels, or were devoted to a particular religion, but others did not. Like increasing numbers of people today they believed in *something* but they weren't sure what. There were also those who, until their experience, believed in nothing at all. I'm extremely grateful to everyone who contributed their story to this book by whatever means. It's a privilege and an honour to share these deeply personal stories with a wider audience. I sincerely apologize if your story isn't here. It's simply because time and space would not allow me, this time . . .

The miracle of healing

Healing and reassurance are the key words that emerge time and time again when people encounter healing angels in their lives. Sometimes there is a flicker of fear and uncertainty at the strangeness and unexpectedness of it all, but these feelings are nearly always overtaken by feelings of peace and comfort. In each and every one of these miraculous stories of healing from the inside out – or, in some remarkable cases, from the outside in – connection with angels provided the recipient with a healing strength, courage and power they didn't know they had.

I sincerely hope that reading the pages that follow will likewise inspire you to become more than you ever thought you could be. I hope it will show you that angels are real and that ordinary people, like you and me, can silence the chatter of noise and fear in their heads and hear the clear voice of an angel calling out to them. Above all, though, I hope the stories will touch your heart, awaken your dreams, heal your spirit and give you wings.

An Angel
Healed Me

CHAPTER 1

An Angel at My Bedside

The unexamined life is not worth living
Socrates

'Your father has passed through casualty,' an impersonal voice said on my answerphone. 'You need to call this number immediately.'

My father died eight years ago, leaving me with feelings of hurt, anger, loss, guilt and relief. There can be no deeper wound than abandonment by a parent. After close to thirty years of distance I was ready for healing, even thinking about re-establishing contact with my absent father, but when I returned that call I was told he had died; it was too late. The wound would never heal. I would have to live with the hurt and the rejection.

More than a hundred people attended my father's funeral. I wasn't one of them. You see, I'd never had a civil relationship with my father. Although my mother told me that when I was very young my father did care for me in his way, I can't remember a time in my life when there was love and laughter between us. I never understood what was going on in my father's life and why he found it so hard to give to me emotionally. He was never around and never wanted to spend time with me or said anything positive about me. I was a wounded girl, soon to grow up into a wounded woman.

By my early teens I had convinced myself that my father was an uncaring, ugly man who didn't care for me, didn't love me and didn't want to be a part of my life. A part of me thought this was because I was unlovable, not worthy of being loved or cared for. I found it hard to make friends at school and to believe in myself. I looked at my dad, the man who had made me feel this way, and blamed him for my loneliness, lack of self-confidence, failed relationships, teenage eating disorder and everything else that wasn't going right in my life.

My mum and dad separated when I was in my late teens and just before I headed off to university I cut all ties with him. There wasn't even the token exchange of cards at Christmas any more. When I left university and entered the world of work I felt grown-up on the outside, but deep down my lack of self-confidence and sense of abandonment hadn't gone away. I found it hard to assert myself, believe in myself and understand my life purpose.

Confused and conflicted, I started to take classes and to read books about self-improvement and self-empowerment. One theme kept coming up time and time again: heal the relationship with your father. It became obvious to me that my disappointment in and hatred of my father was affecting my life and my relationships. I was stuck in 'daddy doesn't love me' syndrome and I needed to heal the past. Trouble was, I couldn't heal. I was too angry and too hurt and too frightened to let go of the past. So I clung on to my hatred and my self-doubt. I wouldn't have admitted so at the time but in many ways this negativity defined me. It was my excuse for not becoming everything I could be.

Around this time I also attended course after course in psychic development. I longed to be able to see angels and spirits like my mother had done all her life. I desperately wanted to have the 'gift' but apart from the odd flicker or insight nothing other-worldly ever seemed to come through. This was hardly surprising. I had never levitated in my cot when I was a baby and I wasn't one of those children who saw dead people in the play-ground, or anywhere else. Growing up I couldn't read people or predict the future.

I'd always known that my mum and grandmother and my brother were psychic, because talk of spirits and angels was com-monplace in my family, but it wasn't until I was in my early teens that I asked my mum what being psychic really meant. She explained that it meant she knew things about people without being told. She could sometimes see and hear angels or see things happen before they took place. She could also talk to people who had passed over. When she talked about her gift I knew in a heartbeat that this was it. This was what I thought I wanted for myself. The problem was, however hard I tried I couldn't have it.

From that point onward, I started reading whatever books I could find on ESP, witchcraft (which was pretty much the only thing around in the 1980s) and the paranormal. My expectation was to see angels floating around, to have the kind of experiences that my mother had. I figured that it was my birthright and that if I kept reading, kept working, kept studying and learning I would have to become enlightened. I joined a spiritualist church and attended the London College of Psychic Studies. I met some wonderful people and mentors. I was hungry for knowledge. At university I was turned on to numerology, crystals and tarot cards, and started performing readings for myself and friends. I knew all the theory about matters esoteric and thought for sure that I would become psychic by doing this. I was wrong. Nothing seemed to work. I wasn't seeing or hearing angels. By the time I reached my late twenties I had finally started to come to terms with the idea that I wasn't, had never been and may never be psychic. I didn't have the gift. I was ordinary. It was another devastating blow to my self-esteem.

For as long as I could remember, self-confidence had always been an issue for me. School playgrounds were a terrifying place and parties or social engagements a nightmare. Perhaps my insecurity was due in part to the fact that Mum's work as a psychic counsellor meant that we never stayed long enough in one place for me to build any firm friendships. Perhaps it was due to the fact that my father was partially disabled and unable to hold down a full-time job, making Mum the breadwinner and constant arguments in my family the order of the day. Perhaps it was down to the fact that we had very little money. Perhaps it was because of my failed relationship with my father or perhaps it was because of the eating disorder that robbed me of my teenage years. Whatever the cause or trigger, low self-esteem was a running theme in my life that limited my chances of happiness and success.

One of the hardest things to deal with in life is change. Sometimes it is just easier to go on as you are, because that's what you are already familiar with and accustomed to. To change means confronting your fears and letting go of the past. It took me close to thirty-five years to take that big step and finally break out of my shell of self-doubt and fear. And the trigger for this remarkable breakthrough was my father's death.

In the hours after I received the phone call telling me that my father had died alone on the doorstep of his house, time seemed to stand still. The day limped past in a blur of tears and confusion and that evening I fell into bed exhausted. For reasons I could not understand, because there had never been closeness between us, the tears would not stop flowing. I lay there crying and crying. I'd hoped that I'd feel stronger the next morning, but if anything I felt worse.

My pain was not rational, reasonable or predictable. It was terrifying for me to feel so out of control. I wasn't usually an emotional person. I found emotions messy and frightening. Even as a child whenever I felt sad or frightened I would find comfort in rising above my emotions, tidying them away in my mind. I couldn't understand my reaction now because I had rarely spent any time with my father and a part of me hated him still. Why was I crying over someone who meant nothing to me? I couldn't forgive him for deserting me. I couldn't forgive him for the way he had treated my mother. I couldn't forgive him for letting me down and for not understanding me or being there for me.

The strength and depth of my grief terrified me and humbled

me. I'd hated my father for so long and had cut him out of my life and my heart, so I wasn't prepared for the sense of loss and loneliness I now felt. I guess a part of me had always longed for some kind of reconciliation – for him to tell me how much he loved me and how proud he was of me – but that chance had now gone forever. His death reopened old wounds and brought everything back to the surface.

My mother's death a few years before my dad's had been terrible to handle because the bond between us had been strong. I had loved my mother with every fibre of my being, but I had never felt the same about my father so I was dumbfounded by the waves of grief that took over me now. Like childbirth, the pain activated something deep and primal within me and filled me with anguish, longing, anger, guilt, depression, despair and unbearable, gut-wrenching pain.

My brother and my father's family organized his funeral. I didn't attend. I couldn't attend. He had never been a father to me and I was not ready to behave like a daughter. My brother told me that more than a hundred people paid their last respects. He told me that my dad must have been very popular. He had devoted many years of his life to good causes and green issues. This just made things even more unbearable to me. My father clearly had love and time to give to other people: so why, then, could he not give it to me, his family, his nearest and dearest?

A week after the funeral I still felt as if a knife was ripping through me. I'd cry at inappropriate moments and my concentration was poor. I couldn't move forward. My father had stopped me dead in my tracks. I knew that I needed help but I didn't know where to turn. And then one night I finally got the answers and the healing I had been longing for.

On that night I fell asleep and started to dream, but it was one of those very clear dreams when you kind of know you are dreaming but can't wake up. It felt wonderful and peculiar at the same time. In my dream I found myself asking to see my father – and then I saw him. I saw him sitting on the bedside of a little girl looking at the pictures in a fairytale book. It was a book I recognized because I had always loved it as a child. It was called *Far and Away*. It had very few words but the pictures were full of magic and colour. The little girl was me and I could see her laughing and pointing. Then my dream changed. I saw my father in front of a huge chalkboard. I saw him write three letters on the board: A, S and D.

I woke with a start at about three o'clock in the morning. I could hear my alarm clock ticking. For a brief moment I felt peaceful and free but then the sadness returned. I was wide awake and I knew it would take ages to go to sleep again so I got out of bed and went to the kitchen to make a cup of tea. When I got to the kitchen my heart stood still when I saw lying open on the table the fairytale book I had seen in my dream. I'd kept it all these years because I had loved it so much but it had been stored deep in the basement, with other memories of my childhood. What was it doing here?

I peered down at the open page and saw the date 9/6/69 scribbled on the top right-hand side in very tiny, neat handwriting. Then I looked at the next page and found another date written in the same place on the page. It was the same through-out the whole book. How could I not have noticed them before? As I looked at the date a memory flashed into my mind; a memory I didn't even know I still had, of my father writing down the date he had read a story to me for the first time. A chill of excitement and uncertainty ran down my spine. Was it possible that my father in spirit had placed the book there? And what about the chalkboard and the letters A, S and D – what did all that mean? My mind raced. Was it possible that in death my father, who had always been absent in my life, was trying to reach me, to tell me something I needed to know?

I was fizzing with an unfamiliar energy and excitement, and my instinct as a paranormal researcher was to immediately switch on my computer and do an online search for 'ASD' or dream meanings of chalkboards or anything that I had seen in my dream. I can't recall exactly what I read but the very first heading that came up contained information along these lines:

> Adults with Autism Spectrum Disorder (ASD) often go untreated and undiagnosed because Autism Spectrum Disorder is generally considered to be a children's illness. Common characteristics of the condition include: being unsociable, mood swings, emotional rigidity, obsessive behaviour and sensitivity to light.

In that moment I got the answer to a lot of questions. As I read on about the symptoms of autism and how it often goes untreated and undiagnosed in adults, especially in its mild form, it was as if my father was being described to me. The way he used to yawn and fall asleep when my mum tried to talk to him. His obsession with numbers and counting and putting little notes and dates everywhere. How everything had to be on his own terms. His emotional rigidity and inability to enter my world contrasting with his compassion for good causes and people who were not emotionally dependent on him, as I was. All those years of blame, hurt and pain. They had been for nothing. I had resented my father and developed such insecurity about our relationship but none of it had actually been his or my fault. If I had only been willing to open my eyes and see what was perhaps blindingly obvious I might have spared myself years of hurt, guilt and pain.

There can be no deeper wound than being abandoned by a parent but I had not been abandoned. For the first time in my life I saw my father in a completely different way. He was the man who had given me life and who had tried to cope as best as he could. When I was very young he must have found it easier to relate to me because I was open and accepting of whatever he could offer, but, as I grew older and started asking questions and wanting more from him than he could give, he couldn't cope and shut me out.

This was a lot to take in and my eyes started to feel heavy. Before I knew it my head was on my keyboard. I drifted off to sleep and had another vivid dream. In my dream my father was standing on a bridge. I was with him. We didn't speak. He picked up some tiny stones and threw them over the bridge into the river. We watched as the stones created tiny ripples that were quickly washed away by the current. Then my father handed me some stones. I threw them in and again watched the ripples disappear.

When I woke up I could feel my father's presence all around me. With images of my dream still ringing in my head, I felt like we were sharing a moment of time and space together. My father was reminding me to let go of heavy stones from our relationship and the pain that rippled through my life. He was urging me to release it to the healing stream of life.

I forgave my father that night. I let go of him and recognized that the past was as it was. There was nothing I could do to change it. All I could do was change the present and build a new relationship with my father in spirit, a relationship built on a foundation of forgiveness of old hurts. I also knew that I too had made mistakes and I asked my father to forgive me. Even harder was forgiving myself. I had been unable to recognize my father for who he actually was and who he could never be. I hadn't seen past myself and my feelings of abandonment. I hadn't understood that being part of a family isn't just about parents providing for their children; it is about being part of a group or team effort where everyone looks out for each other.

There is an amazing, life-changing and healing power in forgiveness. Forgiving my father and forgiving myself that night helped me finally let go of any blame and guilt. It also helped me to understand that with the power of forgiveness at work in my life anything was possible. Soon after healing my relationship with my father in spirit, and accepting him for who he was, my life improved in a dramatic and magical way. Not only was I able to relate better to my own children with trust, acceptance and openness but also any residue of self-doubt and self-hatred that was holding me back vanished. I was finally able to accept others and myself.

The unfolding of an inner relationship with my father has been the most astonishing healing gift from my angels. He has lived on within me through death. In my dreams and in my heart he loves and comforts me in a way he never could in life. He is also wiser and when I ask him for advice about challenges I'm facing in my daily life he can give me a sense of perspective by helping me see the invisible connections between everyone and everything. We often meet in my dreams, where he is free from the limitations and lack of empathy for those dependent on him in some way that consumed his life. After his death and within me, he is at peace with himself.

In the weeks following my father's death I talked to my brother and other family members about my father, really talked. Of course, there was no way of proving that my father had been mildly autistic because so many cases go undiagnosed, but we all agreed that it was a possibility. I also came to understand that the angels chose my dad for me exactly as he was and that establishing a relationship with him in spirit was another wake-up call from the afterlife. I looked back on my life and could see that gifts from the angels had been showered on me in hunches, coincidences and dreams. I just had not been able to see them for what they were. There had been moments of clarity before, when I thought I might be getting somewhere and that the angels had not abandoned me, but nothing like this – nothing as obvious to me in its supernatural origin and power.

Throughout all those years when I had thought I wasn't spiritual or making progress with my psychic development I had been deluding myself. I did have the gift, all along. I just hadn't been able to accept it because I was looking in all the wrong places. I had been looking for it in books, courses and workshops. I had been looking for it in my relationships with men. I had been looking for it in my career. I had been looking everywhere but the one place it could be found: within myself. And the reason I hadn't looked there was because I thought, felt and believed that I was worthless, insignificant and mediocre.

Healing my inner relationship with my father gave me the sense of self-worth I had been lacking. It hadn't been the love of my father that was absent; what had been absent was the love within myself, the love that removes fear and doubt. It had been fear, not my father or my lack of psychic ability, that had held back my psychic development; fear of my own power and my own possibilities.

Until I was able to understand the way in which fear blocks the angels from getting close and in which doubt stops angels speaking, I couldn't fully understand what the angels were trying to tell me. Before they could speak to me I needed to trust in myself and relax. I needed to stop trying so very hard. I needed to find a still and quiet place within me where I could listen to my heart instead of forcing and questioning it.

As I write this chapter I can't help but wonder how many other people there must be out there who, like I did, yearn to see and hear angels and who think there might be something wrong with them because they can't. I want to ask all these people how they can be so sure that they have never seen or felt an angel. Remember, angels don't tend to appear in the traditional manner. Perhaps, like I was, these people have been entertaining an angel unaware and the only thing that is 'wrong' is that they need to become more aware of the subtle ways in which angels can weave their magic and wonder throughout our lives. Perhaps a hunch or gut feeling has led you in the right direction? Perhaps a dream has provided you with insight? Perhaps a kind stranger appeared at just the right moment to be of service at a crucial time in your life?

Angels are spiritual creatures and during my many years of research and interviews with countless people who believe they have seen angels it has seemed to me that angels take the form that is most acceptable to the person to whom they are appearing. You might not think you have seen a figure bathed in light and glory, but that doesn't mean that angels have not been involved in your life and aren't involved in your life right now.

Over the years since I've become aware of angels working in my life and my father returning to live in peace within me, I've noticed huge and important changes in my life and in my psychic development. Everything has just started to make sense and come together. As far as my writing was concerned, for years I'd already been researching and writing about the paranormal but, increasingly, collecting angel stories became my passion. And it wasn't just stories of emotional or spiritual healing that reached me. I also began to collect amazing true stories of physical healing. It soon became clear to me that the angels were speaking to me and guiding me to collect these stories and then share them with others. I found my life purpose, and then came my way the incredible honour and privilege of writing this book to add another voice to the growing angel movement. When people ask me how it has all happened, because I'm no celebrity and don't have a TV show or newspaper column to promote my writing, I tell them it's in the hands of the angels.

Yes, I believe angels are guiding my life and writing but this isn't to say I don't ever have doubts and insecurities any more. Sure I do. I often wonder if I am doing the right thing, or if my angels are hearing me, but I take comfort from knowing that my fears and doubts are entirely normal. In fact, psychologists have a name for this fear and that is 'the impostor syndrome'. Research shows that even the most successful and clever people lack self-belief at times, but this doesn't mean they are worthless. It just means that ego, which is entirely fear-based, is trying to distract them from remembering who they are, from reconnecting with their angelic birthright.

There's a beautiful idea that when a baby is born an angel touches the spot just above that baby's lip, the groove known as the philtrum. According to Jewish lore God sends an angel to each womb to teach babies all the wisdom that can be obtained. Just before each unborn baby comes out, the angel touches it between the upper lip and the nose and all that it has taught the baby is forgotten. Other stories say that the philtrum is an indent left by the finger of God. Similarly, in other folk traditions, it is said that an angel hushes the baby in the womb – to stop it from talking about heaven or to forget both heaven and the secrets told by the angels – and that the philtrum is the spot where the angel put his finger to do so. The reason for wishing the baby to forget is that if he or she brought memories of the love and comfort of the spirit world into this world he or she would want to return. The philtrum allows humans to express a wide range of lip motions, which enhances both verbal and non-verbal communication. Once again this reminds us that it is in our emotions and in our heart that reminders of our angelic birthright can be found.

In the past I couldn't resist my ego-based doubts and fears. I allowed them to trample over my feelings and rule my life. What is different now is that with the help of my angels I have learned the importance of letting go, of not holding on tight to mistakes I may have made or negative thoughts I might have about myself. I have learned to not be frightened of my feelings, to acknowledge and feel them even if I don't understand them, because they are messages from a higher realm. I have learned that low self-esteem and fear block the love and light that my angels want to give me.

Best of all I have learned that, even though I have many flaws, to the angels that love and watch over me I am perfect just as I am. And because the angels see only what is good and pure in my heart I'm able to see what is good and pure in everything and everyone, including myself. I am able to learn and grow and change from setbacks and disappointments and not be savaged by them. I am able to believe in miracles instead of hoping for them, because I know from my own experiences that there are some things in life that just can't be explained. I'm able to come to terms with the fact that, for reasons I may never understand in this life, sometimes horrible, cruel and unjust things happen to innocent and good people; and, even though I can't always do anything to help, the forces of love and goodness will always be more powerful than the forces of darkness. I've stopped trying so darn hard and am finally able to trust and let the angels guide me through this life and the next. The relief after years of yearning and hoping for spiritual awareness but feeling like I was not getting anywhere is exquisite.

Reuniting with my father in spirit was one of many breakthroughs in awareness I have had. There have been many other angel encounters in my life, some of which I have been able to recognize only with the hindsight and the wisdom that comes with age, but space prevents me from including them all here. I just hope that sharing some of my psychic journey with you at the onset will help you get to know me better before I open up my case files for you in the following chapters. I hope as you read on that you will be as comforted and as moved as I never fail to be by the stories of remarkable angel healing I've gathered together for you in this book. The first few chapters will focus more on physical healing or stunning recoveries that science can't explain, while in later chapters we move on to stories of transformation and inspiration, the healing power of prayer and near-death experiences.

Angel stories are proof that goodness is both around us and within us and that we are being noticed, all the time. They are also proof our life on earth is interlinked with the greater world of spirit, a world beyond our understanding but a world that we all can connect to through the healing and bonding power of love. So, as you turn the pages, be prepared for the unexpected. A chill of recognition may overwhelm you, your eyes may fill with tears of clarity, or the hair on your arms may suddenly stand on end as the answers to questions you've always asked suddenly become obvious.

And just one more thing before you read on. If you have any healing angel stories of your own, I'd like to encourage you to share them with other people. As you've seen from my experiences, angel encounters come in so many different guises, and they often appear in the ways we least expect or don't recognize at the time. I didn't exactly see an angel the night my father died but I have no doubt now that an angel did appear in my dreams; and when I was a little girl there he was at my bedside, even if I didn't recognize him. If you aren't sure whether or not you have seen or felt an angel, or heard an angel calling out to you, trust your heart: it will let you know. Don't make the same mistake as I did and let fear and doubt prevent you from feeling, trusting and sharing. Instead open your mind and your heart and see what goodness and love there already is all around and within you. Remember, the more you look, trust and believe, the closer to earth the angels will fly, bringing with them their pure, healing love.

CHAPTER 2

Manifest a Miracle

Never give up on anybody; miracles happen
every day

H. Jackson Brown Jr

You've probably heard stories of people who believe that angels
are guiding their lives and healing their hearts and spirits, but
you've probably heard far less about angels that can actually heal
in the physical sense of the word. But such miracle healings are
possible and you don't need to refer back to biblical or ancient
times to find examples of them. In fact, it's quite possible that
miracles are still happening all over the world today, and that
what appears or is reported to be a stunning recovery from illness
or injury might instead be nothing less than the work of an
angel.

In my research I have come across many stories of individuals
suffering from acute cancer, heart problems, deafness, blindness,
migraine headaches, fevers and so on who experienced miraculous and often unexplained healing. Sometimes these miracles

come via ancient methods, such as the laying on of hands, prayer, affirmations or journeys to sacred places, and sometimes they come from human hands in the form of doctors, nurses, dentists, therapists, counsellors and others – each and every one a miracle worker. In my opinion healing is healing and no less miraculous if it comes through the divine healing gifts given to humans. The means of healing is not definitive. The love and the power of the angels are limitless and can come from countless different methods and means.

Perhaps it is best to consider any form of healing as a blessed gift or mystery that should not be solved but should be welcomed with gratitude. I do hope that the stories you're about to read will inspire you to believe in miracles, both for yourself and for others.

I've had my own experience of an unexplained recovery early in the year while I was busy working on this book. All of a sudden major head pains made my life a misery. For days on end I woke up each morning with a dull ache that by midmorning had become a full-blown headache and by the evening just keeping my eyes open caused me pain. The pain got so bad that I made an appointment with my doctor, who suggested that I get my eyes tested. I did so and there were no problems there. I was referred to an optometrist who ran a series of tests. He could detect nothing wrong with me and simply suggested that long hours working on the computer, combined with stress, might be causing the pain. I cut down on the time I spent at my PC and took better care of myself. The pains didn't fade. It was horrible. This went on for sixteen days.

Unable to work on my computer and with the deadline

ticking away for the completion of this book, I begged my angels to help me. I didn't want my poor health to stand in the way of this book being published and all the people waiting for their stories to appear in print. I'd made a promise to them that I would share their remarkable experiences with a wider audience and I couldn't let them down.

Later I sat on my sofa with my head in my hands and a cold flannel on my head. The pain had reached unbearable levels and I decided to go to my medicine cabinet to get yet more ibuprofen. I never got there, though, because as I tried to get up from the sofa the flannel I was holding on my head felt incredibly heavy. I tried to get up but it was as though something or someone was pushing me back down into the sofa. The sensation wasn't rough or violent in any way, just a gentle but firm push. It took me by surprise and I remember trying to push back against it. In an instant the heavy feeling was gone and I could finally get up. As I stood up and rubbed my head I realized that the pain had completely gone – within twenty-four hours of making my heartfelt prayer – and it hasn't returned since. Had an angel healed me? It certainly felt like that to me. I can't think of any other explanation.

Think back on your life. Perhaps there have been moments when you've suddenly experienced a surge of energy for no reason at all during the day. Or perhaps you've recovered from a bout of illness far sooner than you or anyone else thought possible. Or perhaps you've prayed for the recovery of a loved one and your prayers have been answered. You may not have thought in terms of miracles when it happened, but perhaps these moments were small miracles and you just didn't realize it. Wondrous things really do happen every day.

The dictionary defines the word 'miracle' as something that appears to be unexplainable by the laws of nature. In other words, it's something we simply can't understand in a straightforward sense. Albert Einstein once said that there are only two ways to live your life. One is as though nothing is a miracle. The other is as though everything is a miracle. Today we tend to favour the former, 'nothing' option. We live in a fact-driven world. We need evidence before we form opinions and dismiss events that can't be explained logically. And then every so often we hear about something truly remarkable occurring and for a moment even the most sceptical minds are confused and confounded by what can only be described as a miracle.

That is exactly what happened back in September 2008 when a lady called Colleen Banton talked to the press about her belief in miracles and that an angel had saved her teenage daughter from certain death. The story was widely reported in the US media at the time but for those of you who missed it, here is a brief recap:

Indisputably an angel

Fourteen-year-old Chelsea had a history of complicated health issues. She was born five weeks prematurely with developmental disabilities and had battled serious health problems all her life. She was particularly susceptible to pneumonia and in September 2008 she lay dying of it in a hospital room in Charlotte, North Carolina.

Told that there was no hope for Chelsea, her mother Colleen instructed doctors to take her daughter off life-support and thus allow nature to take its course. Then, as she watched her daughter fade away, an image of bright light appeared on a security monitor. Within an hour, Chelsea began a recovery that doctors are at a loss to explain. Colleen believes that the bright light was the image of an angel and that the apparition saved her daughter's life. 'It's a blessing,' she told NBC News. 'It's a miracle.'

Colleen took a picture of the television monitor on which the image appeared. Some who have looked at it have described it as a flare of reflected light. Others – including nurses who were on duty at the time – say the three vertical shafts of light are indisputably an angel.

At the time Colleen's story sent the media, academics and scientists into a frenzy of speculation and even sceptics were forced to reconsider their cynicism after reviewing the photo evidence. Was Chelsea healed by a visitor from another dimension? I believe that she was.

It will probably come as no surprise to you to learn that I believe Chelsea Banton was visited by an angel. It will probably also come as no surprise to you to learn that I believe wholeheartedly in miracles and recognize that certain things can happen that defy the laws of nature. Even the most sceptical of people may sometimes have moments when they wonder if this earthly life is all there is. There is another level of reality, another dimension, a spiritual dimension. Anyone who has trouble accepting this idea might want to think about radio waves. We know the waves are there, even though we can't see, feel or touch them. Like radio waves, a spiritual dimension also exists and when we are able to tune into it miracles can happen. Angels are messengers from that dimension. Indeed the true meaning of the word angel is 'messenger'.

Colleen Banton's story was the exception rather than the rule, because an image was captured and recorded photographically so the press and media had the so-called proof they crave. In most cases, though, when an unexplained healing occurs there is no such evidence or proof, just personal testimony. However, to those who have encountered an angel that healed them in some important way no proof is needed, because their belief in the reality of their experience is so strong.

Grace doesn't have any proof of her angel experience but there is no doubt in her mind that an angel healed her body. Here's her story:

Heavenly music

I had this cough that just didn't want to go away, even after I'd gone to the doctor three times and taken enough medication to sink a battleship. No medicine helped me. I just coughed and coughed. It got really, really bad. It's exhausting coughing all the time. Every cough hurt, shook me up and my body got weaker and weaker. I had this cough for nearly four weeks.

One day I was sitting in my chair when I heard this music. I listened and could not work out where the music was coming from. I went into my living room to see if I had left the TV on. I hadn't. I went into the kitchen to see if the radio was on. It wasn't. I opened the front door to see if the music was coming from outside. The strangest thing then happened: as soon as I opened my front door there was silence, but when I closed it the music started again.

How can I describe the music? Well, I can't really. It was beautiful, of that I am sure, but I can't tell you what instrument was being played or even if there were voices singing. I think I could hear bells ringing but they didn't sound like any bells that I have ever heard before. I went upstairs into my bedroom and the music seemed even louder than it was downstairs. Again I checked for the source but could find nothing. The experience didn't frighten me at all. It made me feel electric. My instinct was to dance to it, so I flung my arms into the air and started to leap about. It was a good job my sons weren't in – they would have really freaked out at the sight, as I've never been very co-ordinated. But for that brief moment I was Darcey Bussell.

I don't know how long I danced, but when I stopped the music stopped with me and my cough had gone. The cough has not returned. I have never in my lifetime had such an experience as that, and it was a beautiful one. I always used to wonder what goes on in heaven and now I know. There is music and there is dance.

Scott is also convinced that an angel healed his pain:

Never forgotten

Years ago when I was in my late teens I went to bed one night with this throbbing stomachache. I woke up several times and even called my mum for comfort and advice but nothing helped. It was so painful it made me cry and then, just as I was about to call 999, the pain stopped. I opened my eyes and saw something that looked like a blue and white cloud hovering over me. I was amazed but also relieved. I knew it was an angel. I knew an angel had taken away my pain. My experience has never been repeated but it's something I'll never forget. Just thinking about it has kept my faith alive all these years.

Pippa likewise believes that an angel cured her when she was sick:

Healing light

When I was a child I was not very strong. A sickly child, I was ill a lot. I don't want to go into the details, as I still find it distressing to think or talk about it, but I did have three operations that left me with emotional and physical scars. I wanted to go out and have fun with my friends. Instead for many long months I was confined to my bed.

One evening I tried to fall asleep early. I wanted the day to end and prayed for the next one to be better. When I fell asleep I had this experience. People have told me it was a dream but it wasn't like any dream I have had before or since. It felt so real. I could taste and feel everything in this dream. It wasn't surreal. Anyway, in my sleep I went to a beautiful meadow. The grass was green and there was a river running through it. I put my hand in the stream and the water gleamed and glittered as it ran through my fingers. I could hear birds singing and could feel the sun's rays on my face. I was there.

I was by myself and enjoying the beauty and the sense of freedom from my bed and from pain. The next thing I saw was this brilliant bright light coming from the sky above. At first I crouched down and hid my eyes. The light was so bright. Then, as the light came closer and closer, the brightness faded and I was able to take a look. I saw this figure with wings. I could not tell if it was a man or a woman but I did see long hair tumbling over one shoulder. The hair was purple. It took my breath away. Eventually the light touched my body and as it did this incredible feeling of love shot through me.

In an instant I was back in my bed. I could scarcely breathe so I sat up and reached for the glass of water beside my bed. I felt jabbing movements on my chest. They didn't hurt but they worried me so I called for my mum. She came to me and climbed into bed with me, holding me in her arms. I must have fallen asleep because in the morning when I woke up I was still lying on my mum's chest.

The next day I felt stronger and the day after that I felt better than I had felt in years. In a week I started to get well. When I told my mum about my experience that night she said it was a dream. When I talked to my doctor about my healing he said that he had never seen such a rapid recovery. I asked him if he thought I had been touched by an angel. He looked at me in such a strange way that I pretended I was joking. He wasn't going to believe me. I don't think anyone believes me, but I know that what happened to me was much more than a dream. It cured me. It gave me life. I have always believed that angels exist and this experience just confirmed my belief. There is absolutely no question in my mind that an angel healed me that night.

So often when remarkable healing occurs after a night's sleep the explanation put forward is that the experience must have been a dream, even though the person who it has happened to insists that it was much more than that. Norman, whose story is below, knows he definitely wasn't dreaming when he saw an angel:

Gloria

A while ago now, I think it must be around ten years back, I was working in a care home for the elderly. There was this really sweet
eighty-two-year-old lady called Gloria and I'd always stop and have a
chat with her. She had a wicked sense of humour. Turned out we had
a lot in common, as we were both born in the same town and knew
many of the same places and people. She had been a university lecturer
in her life, very intelligent and well read and I learned a lot of interesting things from her. I worried about her, though, because she was
frail and prone to falls. A few months after I started working at the
home she was rushed into hospital with a suspected tumour. The
tumour was removed successfully but when she returned to the home
she wasn't her usual bright and bubbly self. The personality change was
dramatic. Whenever I tried to talk to her she would turn away from
me. She wasn't interested in anyone or anything. This made me sad.

Then, about a month after her operation, she took a turn for the
worse. Medics were called and Gloria's family were told to expect the
worst. It was heartbreaking to see her son and pregnant daughter-in-
law sobbing at her bedside. We all wondered if she would make it
through the night. But at around nine p.m., when everyone had gone
home, I saw an angel close beside her bed. It had this long white cloak
on and its face was hidden by a hood. When I looked down at its feet
I could see that they were not touching the ground. The sight took my
breath away. I didn't move a muscle because I didn't want the vision
to disappear. I was actually seeing an angel. The rays of the angel were
so bright I wondered why none of the other nurses or care workers
could see them – because when I looked around everyone was going

about their business. This vision was mine. The thought entered my mind that this angel had come to take Gloria home but then I just knew that this wasn't the case. Gloria was going to be all right. Gloria was going to live and see her grandchild.

Gloria did indeed live to see her grandchild. In fact she went on to live for ten more years. Best of all she returned to her normal bright and cheery self. We had many more laughs and chats over a cup of tea and a slice of Madeira cake in the years ahead. The smile never seemed to leave her face and she beamed whenever her son brought in Angela, her little granddaughter. When I heard that Angela was the baby's name I couldn't resist an inner smile. I never told Gloria about the angel I saw. She wasn't a religious person. Once she had asked me about the angel pendant I always wear. I told her that I believe in angels but she told me that as much as she would like to she didn't have the courage to believe in such things. It's comforting for me to know that in spirit she has discovered just how much the angels believe in her.

Why me?

It seems clear to me from the stories I have collected that angels have the power to heal people not just in the emotional and spiritual sense, but in the physical sense too. The theme connecting all the stories in this chapter is that all of those who submitted their stories believe they were physically cured not by doctors or science but by angels. But one question I'm always being asked is: why do the angels help some people, but not others? Why does one old lady survive to see her grandchild and another die without that blessing? Why does one child survive against the odds and another is taken by the angels? Why does one person see the light and find their cancer cured and another die in pain?

I found myself asking exactly the same questions several years ago when I was seconds away from certain death. I had been driving towards a busy junction when I clearly heard my mother's voice telling me to turn right, though I had planned to turn left. My mother had passed several years previously. Unbeknown to me at the time, had I turned left I would have faced certain death in a back-to-back collision involving two trucks, a stray dog and several vehicles. Three people were killed in the accident – and I would have been the fourth had I turned left as I had intended to before an angel called my name.

Later that evening, when I found out about the accident, instead of feeling relief I felt wretched. As I tossed and turned in bed that night all I could think was: why them and not me? I tortured myself with feelings of guilt. What made my life any more important than those of Sam the retired postal worker and Harry and Jane the recently married couple who died that day? There was even speculation in the press that Jane had been pregnant. What did it all mean? So many feelings clashed inside my head and my heart – the gratitude for being spared, the guilt of still being alive and the sorrow for those who had died. Over and over again I asked myself: why them and not me? Where had they gone? Were they all right?

A voice woke me, a voice calling out my name, or perhaps it was a whisper. I sat up and looked around my bedroom but no one was there. I pinched myself and it hurt. I was awake and still

I could hear the voice calling. This really was happening. It was the voice of a woman telling me that her name was Jane and that she was all right and I shouldn't be afraid because everything was all right for me too.

I heard that voice for only a brief moment but it was enough to still my mind and fill me with peace. Like a warm blanket, feelings of comfort wrapped themselves around me. I got up and switched the light on and the feelings of peace and contentment stayed with me. I still have absolutely no idea why I didn't die that day but I felt reassured that Jane and the two others who died were at peace, like me. I also realized that those who had died that day instead of me were simply continuing their spiritual journey in another realm. I felt a new resolve to live each day to the full and to make those in spirit feel proud as they watched over me.

Although I have found my own answer to the 'why me?' question I'm not sure I can answer it fully for others. They will have to find that themselves. All I can say is that our guardian angels know things about our spiritual journey that we cannot and, although I personally subscribe to the 'it's not your time' theory, it is beyond our understanding to know why they intervene in some cases but not in others. The spiritual world does not operate under the same laws as the physical world does. The only thing that connects the two worlds is love, and the stronger our love the stronger the connection between the two worlds becomes.

But the stories I have collected do seem to suggest that angels do sometimes intervene and respond to people who are suffering or ill in some way. Many of those who have been healed by an angel in times of suffering have their faith and their life transformed as a result because they realize, perhaps for the first time, that angels are there when we need them. Mimi's story is a very clear demonstration of this fact:

My secret angel

I'm the last sort of person you'd think the angels would want to help. I used to steal and I've been in and out of prison. I've got four children and am trying to be a good mother to them all. I don't blame my children for running away from me. I've let them down too many times. The reason: I couldn't say no to a drink.

For many years I kept my addiction a secret. I know all the tricks. I'd pour my fix into a coffee cup so there would be no questions asked. My handbag would contain a ready supply of breath fresheners. I'd have secret stashes around the house. At work I knew all the clients who would join in with me for a drink or two during lunch or before lunch or after lunch. The joy I felt when male clients would tell me I could drink them under the table was amazing.

I started drinking when I was seventeen. I didn't drink as a child. Alcohol wasn't allowed in our house because my mum was a recovering alcoholic and drinks were banned. I started drinking when I went out with a couple of friends one night to celebrate the end of our mock exams. I had this crush on a boy in the year above me but couldn't pluck up the courage to speak to him. I found the courage with a drink in my hand and I liked the confident person I became. If only I had known then what I was to become.

I ended up sleeping with my crush that night, so alcohol and sex became closely associated for me. The next morning I felt horrible but memories lingered of the new me I'd discovered the night before. I wanted to be that woman again and again. Getting smashed in my final year at school was fairly easy. My boyfriend would supply me with alcohol secretly. I had the time of my life – alcohol made life seem such fun. It was my secret weapon.

I didn't really lose control of my drinking until I dropped out of university, heavily pregnant with my first child. While I was pregnant everyone hovered around me for the sake of the baby but as soon as the baby was born I was alone again. My boyfriend left me. I didn't have a job and I was still living at home. Mum doted on little Tania, my baby. I think she had already given up on me.

For the sake of my daughter I managed to turn things around for the next couple of years. I met this guy who was really into helping me break my addiction. I loved him and so I tried really hard. I went on to have three more children with him. It was the final straw for him, though, when he came home one day and found me buck naked and drunk with a guy from the garage near our house.

After my divorce my descent happened pretty fast. My husband filed for custody of the kids and I know my drinking was the reason the three I'd had with him went to live with him. Tania, my eldest, was also removed by social services but I was allowed visitation rights. Soon I wanted to drink all day. On more than one occasion the police pulled me over in my car and drove me home.

Mum took me to AA and I attended several meetings. I tried really hard but I couldn't hack it. I would pretend to Mum I was getting better and promise to go and see my kids but whenever visitation day came round I'd break out in a cold sweat. I'd have a quick drink to give me some courage but it was never a quick drink. It ended up being one drink after another. Sometimes I'd black out.

I remember one night stumbling in the street close to where I lived. I can't remember how I got there but I could smell vomit on my jacket. Everything started to swirl around me and I fell down on to my knees. I could see that one of my knees was bleeding but I didn't feel any pain and then everything went dark. I couldn't see anything. I looked to my right and saw an angel carrying a large staff of light. It was about four feet long and a few inches in diameter. She – at least I think it was a she – was beating the staff on the ground beside me. She didn't look at me or even seem to be aware of me. She just kept on bashing the staff on the ground. Sparks of light were darting everywhere. I could also see that her mouth was moving as if she was talking to herself, but no sound came out. I tried to understand but could not make sense of anything she was doing or saying. It was so weird and I wondered if, like me, my guardian angel was losing it. I mean angels are supposed to be full of love and gentleness and here was this angel hitting something I couldn't see.

And then everything seemed very familiar to me. I remembered the savage beatings my father had given me when I was a child. How he had hit me over and over and over again, for reasons I did not understand. How he had hit Mum and my brothers. How violent he was. I didn't want to have these memories so I shut my eyes and shook my head but when I did that they became even more intense. When I opened my eyes I could see scars all over my hands, arms and legs.

I held my hands out towards the angel and she put the end of the rod of light on to them. I could see the dark scars disappearing. The memories of the beating I had stored in my mind slowly began to leave me. It was as if the angel was taking them away and then beating them into the ground in front of me. It was clear that the angel took her work very seriously and her eyes never wavered from her rod of light.

Tears filled my eyes as this healing angel pulled out my pain, my buried and secret pain. Each time the scars and dark shadows left me my angel took them and beat them into the ground. She was destroying the pain, the anger and the blackness that had been consuming me.

I can't remember how long this went on for; time didn't seem to exist. But when I woke up I was in a hospital bed and my mum was holding my hand. I could see that her face was red and sore from crying. The moment I awoke I knew that freedom and a new life were mine. I was shaking with joy and excitement. My slavery to alcohol was over.

I later found out that I had been hospitalized because of alcohol poisoning. I had severe brain damage and the doctors had pronounced me a vegetable. Mum was told that there was no hope for my recovery, even with the best care and medication. I am now completely and fully healed and have no sign of brain damage. I am also a recovered alcoholic and have been for three years. I've gone back to school, am working hard to make Mum and Tania proud of me and have never missed a meeting with my other kids. There's also a new man in my life. It's early days yet, but who knows – he might be the one.

I never told anyone, not even my mum, about my experience. When you are a recovering alcoholic and have suffered brain damage you don't want to talk about visions and things like that because doctors may hospitalize you again for mental problems. I certainly wouldn't get to see my kids. That's why if you want to use this story I need to ask you to change my name and the name of my children so it can't be traced to me. I can't tell you, though, what a relief it is to tell you about it. These past two years I have been bursting to share the feelings of love and joy my guardian angel brought to me and brings me still. For the time being, as far as my close circle of family and friends are concerned, my angel will remain my secret, my wonderful, life-giving secret.

Mimi's story shows that no one is beyond the love the angels. Her angel appeared to her in a spectacular and dramatic fashion but most of the time our protectors are not really seen at all. Instead they communicate their love in subtler ways and only afterwards do we realize that they have helped us.

Lily wrote to me via my Angel Talk email and said she felt compelled to share her remarkable story with me. Like Mimi, she also found help and comfort from the angels when alcohol dependence threatened to destroy her life:

Deeply at peace

I was on my honeymoon and expecting my first child when I realized that my drinking problem was going to make my future a disaster. I'd woken up early craving a drink so I decided to take a walk along the beach. I didn't want to wake my husband so I got out of bed quietly and threw some clothes on.

When I got to the beach and started to walk towards the sea I felt a gentle warm breeze. This was surprising because at this time in the morning I would have expected it to be fairly chilly. I took my sweater off and tied it around my waist. I was determined to have a drink-free day and each time the urge for a drink came I picked up a stone from the beach and threw it into the sea. After about ten minutes I became aware of this wonderful smell. It was like chocolate and vanilla and grapes and flowers, all rolled into one. It seemed to be all around me. It made me feel deeply at peace within myself and it took my cravings away. Then the fragrance disappeared.

I went back to my husband and as I entered the room the fragrance returned. I had no idea where it was coming from but it helped me drift off into a wonderful sleep. The incredible thing is that on the night of the fragrance I developed an instant disgust for alcohol that remains to this day. I can't even stand the taste of it and for more than ten years have never had any desire to have a drink again. It was only after reading one of your angel books that I learned that healing angels often use fragrances as a sign that they are watching over us, so I had to get in touch with you.

This next incredible story is from a lady called Barbara:

Get up and walk

I'd suffered with swollen and painful legs for two years. Sometimes the pain was unbearable but on 15 March 2008 my pain was healed by a dream. In my dream I was in this beautiful place. It was like a wood with grass and streams but instead of trees there were angels everywhere. One of them touched my swollen ankles and told me to 'Get up and Walk.'

I woke instantly and without thinking I threw aside my bed covers and swung my legs over the side of the bed. I didn't feel any pain. Then with images of my dream still strong in my mind I slowly got up, using the stand of the bed for support. I made a few tentative steps and then I let go of the bed stand and walked to my bedroom door and into my daughter's room. She was still awake working on her computer and she could not believe her eyes.

Since then the pain has returned on occasion but never to the extent that it prevents me walking as it did before. I truly believe an angel touched me in my dream and healed my pain.

I'd like to include this next angel-healing story here. It is about an eleven-year-old boy whose mother explains what happened to him:

The pendant

My son, Luke, was diagnosed with cancer when he was only seven years old. For the next three years he suffered as no child ever should with operations and chemo. At times I have to admit I even thought he might be better off dead. It was the suffering. I wished it had been me and not him. Three days after his eleventh birthday the doctors told me that the cancer was now virtually unstoppable. It was progressive and malignant and the size of a tennis ball on his left pelvis. The next few days were pure torture as I watched him fade away.

On the fourth day I woke with a start as I thought I heard Luke calling my name, but when I looked at him he was fast asleep. Something made me look at the table beside his bed. There was something glowing there. I couldn't work out what it was so I got up to take a look. When I got there I saw that it was an angel pendant with the word 'hope' written on it. My sister, who believes in these things, must have left it there when she came to visit earlier that day. I picked it up and it glowed brightly. I took a look around to check there was no light coming in and there wasn't. However, the pendant just glowed brighter. I ran my fingers over the glowing areas and placed it on my son's chest. I don't know why I did this, because I didn't believe in these things.

Once on Luke's chest the pendant continued to glow and then the glowing stopped. The room was completely dark. The next morning when I woke up the pendant was still there. I took it off to see if there were any batteries but could find nothing. Then I sat down to hold Luke's hand and mentally prepared myself for the long and torturous day that lay ahead. I saw Luke slowly open his eyes. He didn't speak but he squeezed my hand so hard that it hurt. Where did this strength come from?

From that day on Luke's hand squeezes got stronger and stronger and within five days he was sitting up and talking. The tumour that had been so prominent before had just disappeared. When doctors examined him they could find nothing. I was told that in rare cases spontaneous healing does occur and that I was very lucky. I didn't say anything but in my heart I know that this was so much more than spontaneous healing. I make sure Luke wears his angel pendant every day.

Nicola also believes that angels saved the life of her child. Here's her equally astonishing story:

My little angel

My daughter, Natalie, suffered from seizures when she was a little girl. The first one lasted only a few seconds but it was enough to convince us that something was horribly wrong. We took her to the doctor who immediately transferred us to a neurologist who ran countless tests and then told us there was little he could do except put her on medication. We were gutted. We could not believe that our little angel, who was only three, would need to take such powerful drugs for goodness knows how long.

My husband strongly objected and wanted to try the natural approach to managing her condition, but I wasn't having any of it. My daughter was too precious and I didn't want to do anything that might put her at risk. After three months on the medication, though, it became clear that we would have to do something because Natalie was suffering badly from side effects of vomiting and headaches. We talked to our doctor again and, much to my surprise, he was sympathetic to my husband's desire to try to treat Natalie naturally. He suggested that we try it for a few weeks but only if Natalie was never left unattended at any time, in case the seizures came back.

We moved Natalie's bed into our bedroom and I never let her out of my sight. After a few days her mood was noticeably brighter and she even started skipping. She'd never done that before. However, I didn't dare hope because I'd done a lot of reading up about her condition on the internet and knew that the stakes were high.

Anyway, about two weeks into this plan I was taking a nap with my daughter in our bedroom one afternoon when I woke up and saw this bright light in my eyes. I was hazy with sleep and at first thought it was the middle of the night and my husband had put a light on to go to the bathroom, as he sometimes does. When I realized that it was still daylight outside I looked around for the source of the light – it was just like a really bright torch – and then I saw him. I looked behind me where my daughter was sleeping and saw the tiniest angel figure hovering beside her. He could have fitted in the palm of my hand. Even though he was small – I say he because he looked male – his face was clear for me to see. He had dark hair, rosy cheeks and eyes that looked like marbles. He was beautiful. I closed and opened my eyes several times to make sure I wasn't dreaming, but each time I opened them there he was, hovering over my daughter. It was amazing, out of this world.

As I looked at him I felt a love so strong that it made me feel weak. I had never felt anything like this before. My change of mood must have startled him because he darted into the air and seemed to vanish in the ceiling. I got up telling myself it had been a dream, but I know for certain it was not a dream. A little angel really had come to see my daughter.

In the days, weeks, months and years that followed, my daughter never had a fit again. My husband is convinced that his natural approach made all the difference. I do think this helped but I also think a little angel helped us. I just want to share this story with you because I know there are so many people out there who think that anyone who believes in angels or who sees angels is crazy; but I saw an angel and I can assure you I am not crazy. I believe that it is a person's heart and not their words or actions that can create miracles. My daughter is sixteen years old tomorrow and very healthy.

Sometimes angels can appear in their traditional form and, although this is comforting, it can also cause feelings of confusion. Like Nicola, many people who have written to me over the years have told me that they worry about sharing their experience with friends and family in case anyone thinks they are going crazy. Sometimes they also worry that their angels might lose faith in them because of their reticence to come forward. I do my best to reassure them that the angels would never be offended by a person feeling unready to go public about their belief in angels. What matters to the angels is what manifests in a person's heart. The angels recognize a person's faith without verbal or external endorsements.

Others, especially those whose lives have been transformed by dreams, coincidences or flashes of intuition, write and ask me how they can be sure if an angel really has been at work. I tell them that the very definition of faith is to believe in something you can't be sure of – and we can never be 100 per cent sure, because there is so much about this life we don't understand.

I also tell them that being unable to prove that something is there does not necessarily mean that that something isn't real or doesn't exist. I remind them that visions of angels are rare and that, even if they struggle to accept that what happened to them was angelic in origin, they should at the very least keep an open mind. To do any less is egotistical and ignorant because no one, even the greatest of scientists, can know everything there is to know. The scientific community would never make leaps forward without intuition and flashes of insight. So, if you aren't sure if you have been visited by an angel, rest assured that your questioning is normal and perhaps the first step on your road to a more spiritual life: it is only by asking questions and challenging assumptions that truths are discovered, faith is justified and any kind of progress can be made.

So as you read this book keep asking yourself questions with an open mind. Then simply wait and see what answer comes to you in the next few days. Sometimes the answer won't come and it is only years later that everything will become clear. But if you have an open mind and use your common sense I have no doubt that one day you will wake up, look back on your life and realize that wonderful things that can't be explained away as coincidence or imagination have happened all along the way. If proof is what you want, you will eventually find it; but before you find it you need to look for it and the place to look is in your heart.

All the people who submitted this next batch of stories had an amazing healing experience that either cured them completely of an illness or gave them the courage and hope to recover or survive. They all deserve a place in this 'Manifest a Miracle' chapter because they prove once again that life, and indeed the afterlife, is full of astonishing and inspiring experiences. We just need to open our minds and hearts and recognize them.

Let's begin with Ruby's story:

An angel on my shoulder

Two years ago I was diagnosed with bowel cancer. Fortunately, it was caught in the early stages so I was able to get treatment – treatment that very probably saved my life. I want to tell you, though, about something incredible that happened to me when I was ill.

During the day I kept my fear and worries about having cancer under control. There was my treatment plan to follow and so much going on with my family that I didn't have time to think. At night, though, my anxiety took over and I would lie there worrying that the cancer might spread, that the treatment would fail, that my kids would be without a mother, that my life would end before I felt I had lived it.

My husband would do his best to console me. He knew how vulnerable I felt when it got dark. Sometimes he would hold me until I was asleep or he would place an arm around me and pat me gently, telling me that I was going to make it and that things would be fine for all of us. Even though they didn't remove all my fears, his support and love meant everything to me and really helped. At least I wasn't alone in all this. I had people who loved me.

However, one night, before another round of treatment, I found it almost impossible to stay upbeat. My husband had tried to comfort me for hours but he wasn't helping. Eventually, for his sake, I lied to him and told him I was okay and then pretended to shut my eyes and turn over to go to sleep. My heart was racing and at that moment I really thought I was going to die. I tried to pray but I couldn't find any words to express myself. Then I felt a reassuring hand on my shoulder. It was warm and tender but also firm and supportive. I turned over to snuggle up to my husband but he was at the edge of the bed, turned away from me. I could tell he was asleep because he was breathing heavily. As I looked at him I still felt this hand on my shoulder.

Feelings of comfort flooded through me. I knew then that I wasn't going to die and that I would pull through this. The fear had gone. The hand on my shoulder seemed to have taken it away. Then I felt myself getting sleepy and when I woke up the next morning I felt intensely alive and energetic. I can't remember ever having had such a good night's sleep.

I knew when I woke up that in both this life and the next I wasn't alone. Someone or something good was watching over me. My worries and fears couldn't compete with that. Two years later I've been cancer-free for ten months. I'm human, so worries about my health and my family still come to haunt me from time to time, but I draw incredible strength from my memory of that reassuring hand on my shoulder.

Elizabeth also believes that the reassuring touch of an angel turned her health and her life around. Take a moment to read her story:

Skin deep

After my parents died within three weeks of each other, I got this horrible skin allergy. It started with itching on the bottom part of my legs. The spots there were so itchy I scratched them until they bled and I was covered in open sores on my calves. Then the rash spread to my arms and my lower back. I tried every cream I could find. Nothing helped. I tried so hard not to scratch but sometimes it was impossible not to. My doctor prescribed antibiotics because he was worried about the risk of infection in the wounds caused by my scratching. Things calmed down for about a week and then flared up again with itching all over the tops of my legs as well as everywhere else. It made going to work and carrying on with my life as normal virtually impossible. I looked and felt like a leper.

My doctor told me to wear cotton clothes and to use only natural soaps and deodorants and fabric softeners. He thought it might be a severe allergic reaction to something I was using every day. He also suggested that it might be dermatitis but each cream or oil he suggested to treat it just made matters worse. I was a walking sore. You have no idea how painful things got for me. Some nights I would toss and turn for hours trying to find a comfortable way to sleep that didn't press on the open wounds.

I was in a horrible place – and this went on for four long and painful months. Then one night I had what I can only describe as a vision. No, I didn't see a halo, nor feathered wings nor a white glowing gown billowing in the wind, but there is no mistaking what I saw. I woke up and saw a woman walk towards me. She looked perfectly normal, very human. There were no bright lights. How could I tell she was an angel and not an intruder? She wasn't walking but rather was gliding towards me. Her feet didn't touch the ground. I didn't feel frightened of her at all. In fact, at the time it seemed perfectly normal that she was in my room. She glided to my bed, rose higher in the air and then sat down on the bottom of my bed. She had brown hair and sharp blue eyes. She didn't look like a supermodel or anything. She was just naturally beautiful. She wore a simple brown shirt and purple skirt and purple flat shoes. I remember all that because she let me study her a while before she started to talk to me.

When she spoke it was like she spoke in a different language but I could understand every word she said. She told me that my skin problems were coming not from outside of me but from deep within me. I

45

needed to remember the happy times with my parents because my parents would never find peace in spirit until I did. Then she lifted her right arm and traced a figure 8 in the air – I still have no idea what that meant – and vanished.

When she had gone my bedroom felt empty and cold. I looked at the bottom of my bed and saw a dent in the blankets where my angel lady had sat. I reached down and touched the dent and it felt warm. I looked at my radio alarm clock and the time was eleven minutes past eleven. I switched on my bedside light. There was no doubt about it: I had not imagined this.

As I drifted off to sleep that night I thought about what my angel lady had told me. I remembered the bitter last ten years with my parents. My mother had lost her mind and control of her bodily functions and I had been her main carer. My dad had suffered from a heart condition so he too had been frail. He didn't need round-the-clock care like Mum did but I worried about him also. Before Mum and Dad got ill and dependent on me and my sister they had been a joy to be around. They had fulfilled their lifelong dream of going on a round-the-world cruise; Dad was indulging his passion for model aircraft and Mum was very active in the Women's Institute. I hadn't had to worry about them at all and was just able to get on with my life. I was able to invest all my energy in my career and rise to the top. And when I hit the top I had this whirlwind romance with a guy I thought was the love of my life.

A year after I got married the health of my parents began to deteriorate and when I fell pregnant with my first child things got steadily worse. I went from feeling on top of the world to feeling constantly drained and exhausted. I tried for a while to keep going with my job –

a job I loved – but with my parents so dependent, and my baby daughter also dependent, I couldn't do it all. My parents weren't so ill that they needed to be in a care home – I couldn't do that to them anyway – but they were a constant worry. Mum did silly things like ordering mobile phone after mobile phone. I went round once and found that she had six. She didn't even know how to use one. Dad started to get anxious about going outside and getting fresh air. He said everything was polluted. He stopped taking out his model airplanes.

Things went on like this for five years. My sister didn't help out much. She had her own problems. It was just assumed by everyone that I was the capable one. I was the one who would sort everything out. Some days I felt like a washing machine that was loaded with too many clothes. Something had to give and that something was my marriage. My husband got fed up of being married to a wife who was constantly tired. He had married a vibrant career woman, not this exhausted worrier I had become.

When I woke up in the morning after my angel vision I got out of bed and my first instinct was to start scratching, but the itching wasn't there. The sores were still there but they were not troubling me. I hadn't been free of pain for months. It was a miracle. I tiptoed into my daughter's nursery and saw that she was still sleeping, so I took advantage of this rare opportunity to take a moment for myself.

I went downstairs and made myself a cup of tea. As I sat drinking it I thought long and hard about my angel vision. I tried to do what my angel had said and remember the happy times with Mum and Dad. I felt myself smile as I remembered Dad flying his model planes. He never quite mastered the art but had great fun trying. I heard myself laugh as I remembered Mum and I holding hands and trying not to giggle as we crept to the more expensive seats that were still available when we went to watch a West End show. Then I went further back in time and remembered the wonderful childhood I had been blessed with. How my mum and dad had always been there for me, loving me and guiding me.

I realized in that instant that ever since Mum and Dad had died my thoughts had been dominated by the last five years of their lives, when things had been so hard. In my mind and in my heart I hadn't been able to move away from those oppressive and dark memories. The angel lady had told me that my dark thoughts were unsettling for me, and for my mum and dad in spirit. I needed to let go of them and put every-thing in perspective. While all this was going through my mind something else incredible happened. I had this powerful sense that Mum and Dad were standing behind me. I didn't see them when I turned around but I knew they were with me. I knew they were hold-ing hands and I knew they were sending their love to me.

Remembering Mum and Dad as they wanted me to remember them felt like a weight had been lifted from my shoulders. From that moment onwards my skin condition gradually began to ease. It wasn't cured instantly but this was the turning point. Within two months there was no more itching and scratching and the sores had vanished. I have my angel lady and my parents in spirit to thank for that.

Of course, it is possible that Elizabeth's condition might have been cured by a counsellor or even a psychiatrist but I don't think the medical profession would have been able to change her mind and help her understand that her bad mental state was perhaps triggering her skin condition. The more depressed she got, the worse her skin got, and she needed intervention from a higher realm to help her see the way forward.

Nick's story is similar, in that some people may say that his illness was psychosomatic: simply put, 'all in the mind'. Whether this was the case or not, at the time Nick couldn't find a way out until an angel opened a door for him:

The open door

Last April, in the middle of spring – my favourite time of year so just my luck – I went down with this really bad cold. I wasn't that worried at first but it soon turned into flu and when the headaches and blurred vision started I began to panic. I also had hellish pains in my legs and arms, violent nausea and a throat so dry it felt like parchment however much I drank. Two weeks into this I was sent to hospital. I was given test after test but none could determine the cause. My wife consulted specialist after specialist and they all came up with different theories.

One believed my illness was psychosomatic, but psychiatric testing revealed that this was unlikely. Another bandaged me head to toe to ease my pain. That didn't work. I was in so much pain I couldn't even go to the loo myself. I couldn't sleep without drugs. I was so sick that at times I wanted to end it all.

One morning, after I'd managed to get some breakfast down me, I felt my head spin. The room went topsy-turvy and I must have fallen asleep. Suddenly I was standing beside my bed looking down at my sleeping body. My mum was sitting beside me unaware of my other presence in the room. The next thing I knew I was standing in front of a door. The door opened slowly and I was outside moving with a freedom that I had never felt before. I was so happy. What was going on? This wasn't a dream. It was so real.

I floated down the familiar streets of the village I lived in. I saw people going about their daily chores. Suddenly I was aware of this other presence beside me. It was my dad. My dad had died when I was seven so I never really got to know him well, but he was there. We didn't talk. We were just together and our minds were linked. We communicated with our thoughts. I can't remember what we said. Somehow it didn't matter. It was the feeling of love that I remember, a love I had never felt before.

Sounds crazy, I know, but I can assure you I'm not mad. This is what happened to me. I don't blame anyone for thinking I'm losing it. I would have thought the same, if this hadn't happened to me. Anyway, I floated around like this for a while until my father eventually spoke. He spoke in notes, not words, but I understood them even though I don't play any music and anyone who hears me sing will know I'm tone deaf. My father told me it was now time for me to go back. I told him that I didn't want to go back because living was too painful. Then my dad told me I had to go back to prove to others that angels are real.

The next thing I knew I was back in my body. I opened my eyes and Mum was smiling at me. Slowly I moved my legs and stretched out my arms. I sat up in disbelief. I was bursting with energy. I felt so strong. I put my feet on to the floor and started to walk. Then I started to jog around the bedroom. Mum was speechless, and that doesn't happen very often. I looked at myself in my bedroom mirror. My cheeks were red. I was glowing with health. I was me again. With the help of my father in spirit I was whole again. I was no longer trapped in an unhealthy body. I felt like I could do anything.

Reuniting with a loved one in spirit, a full-blown angel sighting, a glowing light, a scent, a breeze, a dream, a vision – there are so many magical ways for angels to speak to us. But sometimes angels choose not to manifest themselves in ways that are often described as 'out of this world'. Sometimes they can appear in ways that are very much of this world, as Jackie's story illustrates:

Miracle worker

Ten years ago when I was on holiday in the States I was shopping at this huge department store when something astonishing happened. I'm writing to you in the hope that you will be able to shed some light on it. My six-year-old daughter was bored with the shopping trip and driving me a bit crazy. I told her off and got her to sit down on the floor beside me while I asked the sales assistant for some advice.

As I was chatting at the sales desk a boxed television set that was waiting for collection just fell from the counter. I still don't know how or why it happened, or if my daughter had been playing with it not realizing the potential for danger, as my back was turned to her at the time. Everything went into slow motion and I watched with disbelief as the television fell and an old man – he was wearing the store uniform, so he looked like a shop assistant – stuck his hand out and diverted the TV set so it just skimmed past my daughter's head instead of hitting it full on. She was quiet for a few terrible seconds and then began to howl and cry in pain.

I panicked. There was some grazing on her head, nothing serious, but the TV set was so heavy it was possible there could still be internal damage. I hugged her and begged someone to call 911 immediately. Thoughts raced through my head. I'd yelled at my daughter just before the accident. I prayed that this would not be the last time I ever yelled at her. I cursed myself for not paying enough attention to her and not having eyes in the back of my head.

While I was hugging my child I felt this tap on my arm. It was the elderly man. I remember he was wearing glasses; not full-lens glasses but those ones with half-lenses in. He asked me if he could help in any way. I was so hysterical I'm not sure what I said to him or even if I thanked him for averting disaster, but before I knew it he had my daughter on his lap and was joking with her. Normally I wouldn't have let strangers touch my daughter, especially an older man like this, but this man had very probably saved my daughter's life. When I was told that the ambulance was outside the old man looked at me and said that I shouldn't worry: she would be just fine. His words had this brilliant calming effect on me.

By now the paramedics had arrived and were giving my daughter a check-up. I turned around to thank the man for being there but he had gone. I did a quick search down the aisles with my eyes as we left the building but he was nowhere. He had vanished into thin air. There is no way that someone his age could have got away so quickly. I had turned my back to him for only a few moments. That day my daughter was x-rayed and, just as the old man had predicted, everything was fine.

When I later returned to the store I asked if there was anyone on the staff who matched his description but drew a blank. Even the sales assistant I had been talking to when the television fell said she hadn't seen him and didn't know who I was talking about. It seems that I was the only one who saw him that day – even my daughter has no recollection of him. I didn't imagine him, of that I am sure. I guess what I really want to know is did I meet my daughter's guardian angel that day or was it just a kind stranger who shunned the limelight?

Later in this book I'll talk more about mysterious strangers appearing at just the right moment to offer assistance and then seeming to vanish into thin air, as well as other earthbound signs, such as coincidences and the appearance of white feathers or other meaningful presentations. For now I'd just like to ask you to reflect on how reading the healing stories in this chapter has made you feel.

Surprise and perhaps disbelief are common responses, especially if you don't feel you have ever experienced an angel healing for yourself. But, even if you don't think you've seen an angel, I'm hoping the stories may trigger feelings of hope and optimism. Hold on to those feelings, however timid, because they are the doors through which your guardian angels can enter your life and make themselves known to you.

Every time I read an angel story it renews and regenerates my connection to the world of spirit. In my life I've been offered 'proof' that angels are real, through supernatural experiences that have been so profound and undeniable they have given me goosebumps. At the time of occurrence these experiences have wrapped me in warm blankets of peace and comfort, but all too often the intense joy I have felt begins to gradually evaporate as I drift back into the routine hustle and bustle of my daily life. Sometimes I find myself questioning my angels again. I'm not alone. Even those who have had the most intense and vivid angel encounters never lose their doubts and fears completely. I guess what I'm saying here is that an angel encounter, although incredible and life-affirming, is not a cure all. It won't stop you ever worrying or doubting again and it won't make your life perfect. This is because the proof angels give us of their existence is not tangible. We can hold on to it for a while but, like sand dropping between our fingers, eventually it slips away. That's why, regardless of whether or not you have had an angel experience, just reading stories of angelic encounters like the ones in this book can draw the healing power of angels back into your life. Perhaps one story in particular lingers in your mind. Focus on that story. It could be the medium your angels have chosen to open your heart and speak.

Whenever they are read or shared, angel stories are miracles helping to reconnect us with the healing power of our angels. Like an angel encounter itself, reading angel stories can stir feelings of love and hope in our hearts and by so doing let the angels in and refresh our faith in the eternal power of love and goodness like a plunge in ice-cold water.

CHAPTER 3

Hospital Angels

Angels are bright lights in the midst of our
lives
                              Author unknown

In the previous chapter we looked at some of the miraculous
ways in which angels can bring healing miracles into our lives. In
this chapter I'd like to draw your attention to stories of events that
took place not in a person's home or other everyday setting, but
specifically in or around hospitals.

When I started writing about angels and collecting stories I was
surprised and delighted by the number of stories sent to me (and
that continue to be sent to me) not just by people who have been
patients in hospital but also by doctors, nurses, care workers and
other hospital staff. I had thought that with their scientific and medical background medical staff would be the very last people to get
in touch, so it was heart-warming to discover that there are caring
professionals out there today with open minds and hearts and a
keen eye for the divine in the midst of human suffering and need.

I guess, having taken the time to really think about it, I shouldn't really have been so surprised by these hospital stories winging their way towards me. Hospitals are challenging and upsetting places to spend time in, for both patients and their relatives and the people who take care of them. Yet it is clear that the very same stresses that make life in a hospital so difficult and emotionally intense can also provide opportunities to experience some of life's greatest wonders and mysteries.

If you've ever spent time in hospital or visited a patient there you may perhaps have encountered some of this belief in angels of death, comfort and healing held by patients as well as by nursing staff and doctors. I've spent time in hospital for various minor ailments and have come across it for myself during my conversations with staff and from witnessing the behaviour of other patients. I didn't have to look far to find angel symbols and belief in angels among both patients and carers. Indeed, after the publication of one of my previous angel books I received an incredible letter from Charlotte, which I'll share in part with you here:

Flying colours

The day after I got your book I had an appointment at the hospital for a hearing test. I was shown into a waiting room where there were forty people waiting to be seen. The lady who sat next to me told me I was in for a long wait. Then a doctor came into the room and called my name – a little miracle, don't you think, given the amount of waiting I usually have to do at surgeries. When I walked over to him, he shook hands with me and said, 'How nice to meet you; please come this way.'

While he was testing my hearing, I noticed a book lying face down on his desk. I was curious because the colouring of the book looked very familiar so when the test was finished I asked him if I could see the title – and sure enough it was your latest angel book. I asked him if he had read it yet. He said he hadn't but he had heard everyone in the hospital talking about it. He passed it over to me and asked me to have a look. The page it opened on was the very page which had my name on and the newspaper story I had sent you about a little girl's letter to her father in heaven. He then told me that he thought these books were delightful and very popular in this hospital. I thanked him and told me I would pass his comments on to the author. By the way, I passed my hearing test with flying colours.

I wrote back to Charlotte to thank her sincerely for passing this information on to me. Again her story did not surprise me. I once interviewed a group of twenty nurses and more than half of them told me they thought they had seen an angel at some point in their hospital careers.

The following account was from a remarkable lady called Laura:

My silent angel

What happened to me changed my life forever. About four years ago I was diagnosed with anxiety, post-traumatic stress disorder and manic depression. I was in and out of hospital for a few months. The doctors and specialists just didn't seem to help and eventually they wouldn't give me any new medication to try. They'd run out of answers. It was like a big black hole. I was sinking deeper with each day that passed. I just couldn't seem to break free from that dark circle.

Then, on 25 March 2005 (I'll never forget that night), at about two a.m., I was sat on my bed in my dorm, wide awake. I couldn't sleep and was sitting there cold, alone. I was scared and believed there was no future for me. Then the most amazing thing happened. I felt a sudden rush of warmth, as if someone was hugging or comforting me. To my astonishment, in the mirror opposite my bed appeared to me what I can only describe as a beautiful but silent angel.

Her presence was divine: the most beautiful eyes you have ever seen, flowing and golden curly hair. All around her was an aura of blue like no colour on earth, like a neon blue, white and purple colour. Her kind, warm and loving touch was amazing, like a reassurance that all was well and there was absolutely nothing for me to be afraid of.

While I was still staring in amazement at this beautiful being, something astonishing took place. She spoke to me not in a physical sense but an emotional sense. She moved her lips and silently said to me, 'Everything's going to be all right.' The whole vision must have lasted about ten minutes.

I don't know why or what made me do it but the ironic thing is that earlier that day I had been to the chapel on the hospital grounds to seek comfort; I had asked God to give me a sign and for guidance. I then went back to my ward thinking no more about the conversation in the chapel. It's like the old saying my grandmother used: if you don't ask you don't get. This has proved to be true for me.

I was allowed to go home the next day and I have never looked back. To this day I truly believe that the angel had been sent from above to love and comfort me when I needed it most. I feel blessed to have had such a wonderful visit from one so divine. Each and every day I can feel the presence of angels; they are around us even if we don't know it. Since this experience I have had a number of visits from all kinds of loving spirits and, no matter where I go in life, there always seems to be guardian angels watching over me and my loved ones. Thank you for letting me share my experience.

Joy is also convinced that an angel visited her, when she was coming down with polio in the autumn of 1941, before the antibody serum had been invented:

Magnificent angel

I was just nine at the time. I saw this mighty angel standing by my hospital bed. She had a white robe on and golden hair and she said that she would always be with me. I remember that there was so much light coming from her that I put my hands up to protect my eyes. I did get very, very ill at one point and my parents must have feared the worst but I did eventually get through the sickness with no paralysis.

While I was recovering I didn't see my angel again but I did feel her presence beside me. I've continued to sense her and I always know it is her, my angel. She kept her promise to me all these years and I've never felt alone.

Alison believes that an angel spoke to her and transformed her life when she was in hospital. Here's her remarkable story:

59

Vanilla ice cones

This story is one that a lot of people, myself included, struggle to make sense of. I'm going to tell you it, though, because it is the story of my life and how it almost ended way too soon.

I was a lucky girl. I was the beloved child of doting and fairly wealthy parents. I lived in comfort and got almost everything I wanted. I had loads of friends and became head girl of my private school in my final year. I got a coveted place at Oxford and followed that up with a job I loved and a man I adored. My health was good too. I guess you could say I led a pretty charmed life.

With so many things going right in my life I never thought about my mortality. I was going to live forever. I delayed having babies until I was thirty and then got pregnant as soon as we started trying. When I celebrated my thirty-fourth birthday I was in a wonderful marriage and had a healthy and gorgeous three-year-old boy called Riley. What I didn't know at the time was that by the time I reached my thirty-fifth birthday my perfect world would be shattered.

Just after Riley was born I suffered from blocked milk ducts and to make sure there was nothing more serious I was sent to a consultant to be given the all clear, which of course I was. The consultant did tell me to be vigilant about checking my breasts, but I was just too busy and happy to worry about things like that. There was no history of breast cancer in my family and I thought I was far too young. Then a few years later I began to feel an uncomfortable heaviness and lumpi-ness on the bottom of my left breast. My husband made me make an appointment to have a mammogram. Reluctantly I agreed to go.

A few days later when my doctor told me that I very probably had breast cancer I felt as if I had just crashed into a wall at 100 miles an hour. My husband was with me but I felt intensely alone and abandoned. So this was it. I was going to die. As we drove home there was an unfamiliar silence in the car, interrupted only by occasional gulps from me.

When I got back home, Riley rushed towards me in his usual manner. I hugged him so hard I think the poor mite must have struggled to breathe. When I finally let him go my face was wet with tears. He wiped them away with his thumbs and then told me the strangest thing. He told me that I should not worry because a vanilla ice-cream lady had told him that although I was going to be poorly for a while I would be fine. I was ill but I needed to fight.

This made me feel anxious because I had told my au pair not to tell Riley I was at the hospital. This was far too much for a four-year-old to take on board. I had also told her to stop indulging his love of ice cream because he was breaking out in spots. The au pair tried to convince me that she hadn't said anything to Riley or fed him ice cream but I didn't believe her. I didn't want her around so I asked her to leave immediately.

For the next half an hour or so Riley kept on talking about the vanilla ice-cream lady and his chattering did give me some much-needed distraction and relief. I asked him who this lady was and he pointed behind me and told me she was standing right behind me. I told him there was no one there but he insisted. I thought he was probably going through his imaginary-friend stage so I went along with it. He got very excited and told me that the vanilla-cone lady was watching us and she wanted me to fight.

I thought my son was just babbling nonsense but as he talked and talked about this invisible lady I felt lighter. The word fight echoed in my head and somehow I didn't feel as helpless and as abandoned as before. I'd heard and read about women who had beaten cancer, so why couldn't I be one of them. I had so much to live for, a loving family to care for me and a life to live. And so began my three-year-long battle with cancer, a battle that included a radical mastectomy, chemotherapy and even a bone-marrow transplant.

I learned a great deal about the innate goodness of my friends and family during this hellish period in my life. Friends and family couldn't do enough for me. It was a long, tough road but gradually I began to feel hope and this hope somehow made me stronger and more positive. The possibility of recovery became a reality for me. I made the decision to quit negative thinking because although it was possible that I might not pull through this it was also possible that I would. Considering my options and that I didn't have anything to lose I made the decision to opt for the positive and it made a vital difference to my emotional and physical health and wellbeing.

Looking back I can see now that my decision to fight and hope made it possible for the angels to come to me. If I had been weighed down with negativity they might not have come through. The first night angels came and lifted me up was when I was confined to bed rest after a course of chemotherapy. I needed a wheelchair to get from place to place and was so weak from the treatment that I had already spent seven weeks in isolation in hospital while doctors tried to find a way to treat my dangerously and persistently low blood counts.

Then one night – I think it was at around eleven because the nurse had done her last round for the night – I lay there trying to fight the feelings of weakness, sickness, nausea and fatigue that were washing over me. I'd been fairly strong up until now but perhaps this thing was getting the better of me. I remember a part of me hoping that in the morning I wouldn't wake up. The fight was leaving me. I had battled long and hard but enough was enough. I closed my eyes and tried to swallow but my throat was too dry. I couldn't even swallow any more.

Wishing the pain away I closed my eyes and saw Riley's lovely face looking at me. The thought that I might not see him grow up was so painful it made vomit come up in my throat. Then, with Riley's smiling image still in my mind, my nostrils filled with the scent of vanilla ice cream.

Suddenly the pain, the nausea and the vomit ceased; everything was gone. All I could feel was a pair of arms gently lift me. I was floating several inches above my bed. I saw bright colours and an exquisite bright white light. There was also a bright violet light, I say it was violet but it was actually a colour I can't describe – I had never seen it before.

I couldn't hear or see anything but I felt invisible hands stroking me and touching my forehead. I also sensed the presence of love and joy all around me. It was like there was a party or family reunion and I wanted to get up and join in with the laughter. I felt my heart grow larger with an intense surge of hope. It was the most beautiful experience of my life, akin to the feeling I had had when Riley was placed in my arms after he had been born and our eyes met for the first time.

Far too quickly I heard a voice – I don't know if it was male or female – saying, 'You're done.' I felt myself gently being lowered back into bed and then the lights and the sensation of floating were gone. I looked around me and pinched myself. I had not been dreaming. This was the real deal.

Over the next few weeks and months the angels continued to visit me and rock me gently backwards and forwards. I always knew when they were going to arrive because I would smell the heavenly scent of vanilla ice cream. Each time the angels came to me I felt myself getting stronger and stronger. I could feel my life energy returning. It was like the hum or buzz of my being.

Doctors could not believe my remarkable recovery when I left hospital and was finally allowed to go home. I don't know why, but the angels didn't visit me again while I recovered at home; but nonetheless six months later I was given the all clear. I believe the angels leaving me was their way of telling me that I didn't need them any more and that I was ready to recover on my own.

One year on I was back to being my busy, energetic self again, but even though I may have looked similar, inside I felt totally different. There was a depth and richness to my life that hadn't been there before. I never spoke to anyone about my visit from the angels but I did ask Riley if he still saw the ice-cream cone lady. He told me that she didn't visit him any more and he missed her. I told him not to feel disappointed because even though he couldn't see her I believed that she could still see him.

I'm forty-eight years old now and there's no sign of the cancer coming back. Yes, it took precious years out of my life, but looking back I would not have had things any different because I have discovered so much about myself and about life, both this one and the next, as a result of my experiences. And it will always be my honour to feel both joy and sorrow whenever I smell the scent of vanilla – joy because I know there are guardian angels taking care of me but sorrow in that it took being close to death to recognize their loving and constant presence.

Alison's story is a touching illustration of how during times of poor health, when we discover the hard way that whether we live or die is out of our hands, angels can and do draw close to us. This may explain the huge number of angel sightings that occur in or around hospital.

As well as divine sensations, visions and smells, angelic encounters in hospitals often mention bright or shining lights, like those mentioned in Stewart's story, below:

Bright eyes

Nine years ago I had a seizure and was flown by helicopter to hospital; my condition was considered that serious. I went into a coma and came out of it two days later. The amazing thing is I can't remember anything of those two days but I can remember something that happened within a few hours of me coming round.

I looked around my room and I saw these balls of light coming towards me. What was really odd was that when the balls of light came close to me they exploded into a rainbow of beautiful colours. It was like watching a fireworks display. And with each explosion I felt life, energy and awareness coming back into me.

My rational mind has told me time and time again that it was just the aftereffects of the coma, but I didn't just *see* bright lights around me. I could feel them. They were alive. They were active and they were purposeful. I believe they were angels sending me healing.

Diana also saw a bright and dazzling light but in her case it took the form of a figure:

Light falls

Two years ago last September I was in hospital recovering from an operation when a new intake of patients came in. There were two ladies who both came in to have their gall bladders removed. One went down to theatre and a little while later came back to the ward, and then the other lady was taken down. She didn't come back for a long time, and while the first lady had recovered enough for her to go home soon the other lady was very poorly and during the night doctors kept a close eye on her.

With all the comings and goings around this lady's bed I didn't get much sleep as I was in the bed opposite her. Then at one point I became aware of this very bright light shining from her cubicle area. I looked up and I saw this amazing angel hovering above her by the top of the curtain rail around her bed. The angel seemed to be looking down at the lady. The angel was wearing a white long gown; I didn't see any feet but she had blonde hair and fully fledged white wings. I could not see her face as she had her back to me because she was looking at the lady in bed.

I can only think that this lady had her guardian angel watching over her that night because a week later she was well enough to go home (even before me!). I am positive that this wasn't just a dream. I know what I saw and it was wonderful and so peaceful. I shall never forget it for as long as I live.

Mona's story features a misty figure:

The figure wrapped in mist

When my son was little – about seven – he got ill with German measles. The condition itself wasn't too serious but he developed an infection afterwards and became very ill indeed. He vomited every time he ate or drank anything and the fever was terrible – he burned to the touch. I got very scared and didn't know what to think when he told me that he could see things all around him and they had faces.

He was taken to hospital and because his dehydration was so bad he was placed on a drip. That first night in hospital was the longest night of my life. The doctor let me stay over and I didn't sleep a wink. Eventually, though, at about five a.m., I finally succumbed and fell asleep like a log. When I woke up I had to shield my eyes because there was light all around my son. I could not move. At first I felt scared but then my fear subsided as the light around my son started to resemble a figure, a figure wrapped in mist. Then the figure gradually melted away. I got up and ran to my son and saw that he was safe and sleeping peacefully with a hint of a smile on his face.

My son recovered gradually after that and within a few days he was okay to go home. I didn't tell my husband about what I had seen because I knew he would not believe me. I spoke to my son about it and he said he couldn't remember anything but I'm still convinced I saw an angel of healing.

Even though the life of her mother wasn't spared, Denise believes she met her guardian angel in hospital:

My guardian angel

During the week of 26 March 2007 my mother Edna had a stroke and fell into a coma. My sister Chris and I never left the hospital for two weeks; we slept in the room with her and every day we used to go to the chapel and pray that she wouldn't suffer for much longer.

One evening, on our way back from the chapel, we were talking as we climbed a flight of stairs to get to the ward. On the opposite side of the stairs I noticed a gentleman looking at me and smiling; he was very handsome with piercing blue eyes. He looked straight at me and his face lit up. I said to my sister, 'Did you see that man? He had beautiful eyes.' And she replied, 'No love, there was no one there.' When I looked again he was nowhere to be seen.

Soon after, my mother passed away peacefully. I strongly believe that man was my guardian angel looking out for me because after seeing him I felt such a strong sense of peace and comfort.

Georgia told me that she too will never forget her heavenly encounter in hospital:

Electric dreams

I didn't see angels with my eyes. I just knew they were there and it was electrifying.

I was in hospital recovering from my hysterectomy and feeling pretty sorry for myself. I was only twenty-seven and I would never have children of my own. Two months ago I'd been diagnosed with cancer of the womb and my life had come crashing to a halt.

One night, after many nights and days of crying and wondering what the future held for me, I felt I couldn't take it any more. Still sore from the operation, I begged for the pain and thoughts to go away. All of a sudden I felt this sensation go through me. The only way I can describe it is like an electric shock. I was lying on my back at the time and the sensation was so sharp that it made me arch my back. I automatically breathed in deeply and then turned on to my side. I just knew I was experiencing an angelic visitation. It lasted only a few moments and seemed to go through my whole body and then into the bed and the wall behind me.

I must have fallen asleep because when I woke up the next morning I felt like a new woman. I might never have children of my own but there was so much more to life and I was going to live every precious moment of it to the full. The psychiatrist who had been visiting me to talk to me could not believe the turnaround in my thinking. She said she had never seen anything like it. The doctors also could not believe how fast my wound was healing. Again they said they had never seen anything like it.

To this day I know an angel came to me that night and healed my pain and despair. I don't think anything or anyone else could have changed my mind about myself in such an electrifying way.

Angelic encounters can occur in many different hospital settings and situations, but many of the stories I've collected do seem to centre around operations or surgery. Georgia's angelic encounter occurred after her surgery in the recovery period, but Brenda, who tells her story below, believes she actually encountered an angel during her surgery:

Light experience

Back in 2001 – a horrible year for me and the whole world – I was diagnosed with stage 1 breast cancer. I was told that I needed an operation to remove the growth on my right breast. If I didn't have it the chances of the cancer spreading were strong.

After my operation memories of an experience I had had flooded back to me. The first thing I recall was that everything felt soft and clear. I was floating above my body watching the surgeons operate. I didn't feel any pain. I noticed that the time was two p.m. I had a good look around the ceiling and it looked pretty dusty. Then I took myself on a journey out of the room along the corridor. I watched the nurses talking to each other. Then I felt a longing within me to enter a dark tunnel. I couldn't see the tunnel but I knew it was there. Things went a bit fuzzy at that point. I was surrounded by bright light. I was swimming in it. I wanted to melt into it. But then I heard a voice shouting at me to wake up.

I shot back into my body. Things were still fuzzy and unclear but I do recall looking at the clock and it was about four p.m. Then everything went black and the next thing I was aware of was waking up a few days later and feeling sore and very thirsty. Later I realized that the voice I had heard was the voice of my grandfather. He had died two years previously.

Brenda's story sounds a lot like a near-death or out-of-body experience, both commonly reported phenomena in the context of operations and medical situations. They stand in a class of their own and deserve more attention than I can give here so we'll talk more about them in Chapter Six. For now we return to the theme of angelic encounters in medical situations. Simon thinks an angel spoke to him before he underwent surgery:

An angel spoke to me

My father had died from a heart attack at the age of forty-four and with my forty-fourth birthday fast approaching I was terrified that history might be repeating itself. The doctors examined me and decided that they needed to operate to remove some of the blockages from my heart. The day before my scheduled operation I was weak with fear. I didn't want to leave my eighteen-month-old son behind the way my father had left me behind. I remember going to the bathroom and there being this nurse at my bedside when I returned. She helped me back into bed and stroked my arm, saying, 'You will be fine.' I asked her how she could be so sure. She smiled and said that I was loved and I wasn't going anywhere just yet.

I will never forget her and the love I felt coming from her. Her voice was so soft and soothing as she took my pulse and calmed me down. She left just before the nurses arrived to prepare me for my operation and even they were surprised how relaxed I was. I signed the papers and went to my operation with a smile on my face.

When I was able to talk again about what happened I asked my doctor to send a thank-you note to the nurse who had helped me get through the operation. He asked me if I knew her name, but I didn't. He asked me what she looked like. I tried to describe her. I told him she had a soothing gentle voice and was young, slim and had blonde hair and she looked like an angel.

The next day I asked about her again and my doctor told me that no nurse fitting that description had been on duty that night; and because I was being prepared for my operation anyone who came into contact with me would have been noted down on my chart.

I've fully recovered from my operation now and feel as good as can be expected. I celebrate my forty-fifth birthday soon and I intend to celebrate many more. As for the mystery lady in the hospital: yes, you could say that this was a hallucination, but I will never believe that. I think I spoke to an angel and an angel spoke back to me.

Shining lights didn't accompany Simon's angel but he believes nonetheless that he received a visitation from a mysterious stranger or angel in human form. In much the same way as for angelic visions and encounters there are an unusually high percentage of these kinds of experiences reported in hospital settings. Experiences like this one sent to me by Nadia:

Heart pounding

I went into hospital for a completely routine, virtually no-risk procedure but just as I was about to be given an anaesthetic something happened to me that I was dreading. I had a panic attack. Although very rarely, I had suffered them before. I can't breathe and I just want to run and hide. Trouble is, when you're on an operating table there's no opportunity to run. Normally when I'm like this my mum is close at hand. She is the only one who can help calm me down. She rubs my head and holds my hand and talks me into believing I can pull through. But she had been told she couldn't come into the operating room. With the staff lost in their preparation work and nobody looking out for me I was on my own.

I was just about to rip out my IV cord when the doors opened and a young man walked in wearing a mask and scrubs. He noticed what was happening and came up to me and held my hand. He spoke to me in the same reassuring and calm way that my mum does and gently rubbed my head, again just like my mum does, and the fear just left me. I was okay to go ahead.

The nurse and surgeon looked surprised when they turned around and saw this man talking to me. They asked him who he was and he just said he was a medical student trying to help out. He kept on talking to me until I was asked to count down from ten. I can only recall hitting seven.

It wasn't long before I returned home, safe and sound, after my operation. I told my mum about the medical student who had turned up at just the right time to help me and asked her if she had told him how to calm me down. She said she had never talked to a student. I wrote to the hospital to ask them about the students who were in that day. I gave them all the details about my operation – day, time and so on – because I really wanted to thank this guy. The hospital replied promptly via email and told me that there had been no medical students in that day, so perhaps I had been mistaken. They said they did not know who I was talking about. After reading some of your books, Theresa, I think I now know who that man was.

Tania had a similar experience, but in her case the mysterious visitor wasn't a stranger at all but someone very familiar, very dear to her heart:

Staying close

In 1997 my eight-year-old son, Daniel, was diagnosed with leukaemia. He was in and out of hospital for a whole year. One month he went down with yet another infection and had to stay for several weeks at hospital. I stayed close by him, day and night, praying that he would pull through, and that is when something remarkable happened to me, and I believe to him.

One evening at five to ten (I recall the time exactly, for some reason), I was sitting by Daniel's bedside and he was wide awake but I was fighting sleep. I'd been awake since five in the morning. I told him I just needed five minutes' shut-eye and I remember putting my head down beside him on the bed and feeling comforted by him stroking my hair.

Then I heard someone calling my name. I sat up and looked around. Then I looked at Daniel. He was sleeping peacefully. I looked at my watch and it was only one minute past ten. I'd been asleep only a few minutes then. When I looked up from my watch I saw my maternal grandmother standing there. Nothing unusual, you might think, but it is when you consider that she'd died ten years before Daniel was born. She looked really happy and I noticed that her lips looked wet and her cheeks were pink. I tried to stand up to get a better look at her but my feet wouldn't let me. She told me that Daniel would not die, that every-thing would be fine and this would be his last hospital stay for many years. Then my head and eyes got heavy and I felt compelled to rest them on Daniel's bed again.

Moments later I was wide awake. I sat up and noticed that Daniel was wide awake too. He smiled and asked me if I had had a good nap.

I said I had and asked him how his nap had been. He looked puzzled and told me he had been awake the whole time. I looked at my watch and it was only two minutes past ten. In the space of seven minutes I had either had the most incredible dream or I had visited another time and dimension.

This was to be Daniel's last visit to hospital. After that his infection healed and his cancer just faded away. He is now eighteen and completely cancer free. I believe that my grandmother was a guardian angel come to give me hope. If she wasn't an angel how did she know that Daniel wouldn't return to hospital?

In this next story, sent to me by Tom, a mystery stranger brought not only hope but also the gift of life:

The greatest gift

This happened back in 1967. I returned home after a nine-month stint abroad in the army. When I got back I could tell immediately that something was very wrong. My mother was dying. I was furious that no one had told me but apparently it had all been fairly sudden. Only a few days earlier her kidneys had failed and she had been hospitalized. The only hope was a blood transfusion but the problem was that she had a very rare blood type, AB.

All the family, including me, were tested and no match was found. A wider search was begun but nothing came back. We were running out of time and doctors told me that if she didn't have a transfusion soon she was hours away from death.

When I went in to visit Mum she only barely recognized me. We didn't speak – she was too frail – but we did hold hands for a long time. I always knew that one day my mum would die but I didn't feel ready to lose her yet. I wanted to introduce her to my girlfriend. I wanted to make her proud of me. The last time we had parted there had been angry scenes, as she had never wanted me to join the army. How ironic that she had been worrying about me dying and now she was fading away first.

When the doctor told me that we all needed to prepare ourselves for one final goodbye I knew I needed to be strong for everyone else. When you're an army man you become all too familiar with death and the loss of those close to you. My sister wasn't coping too well and I was worried about her so I decided to take her home and then sit with Mum myself.

I took my sister home and then on the way back to the hospital I saw this guy in army uniform standing by a bus stop. It was very late and pouring with rain and something made me drive up to him and ask him where he was going. When he said the hospital I said I was going there too so he may as well come with me.

I was too focused on Mum to talk to him but this man seemed to sense my grief and asked me if I was okay. Without thinking I blurted out the whole story about my mum dying because we couldn't find the right blood type to save her. He listened very carefully and then told me that he was AB and he would do what he could to help my mum.

I nearly swerved off the road when he told me this and just raced to the hospital as fast as I could. Mum got her transfusion and went on to live for another fifteen years. Not only did she meet my girlfriend but she met my sons, Ralph and Ryan, too and spoiled them both rotten with sweets and treats.

I never found out the name of the soldier with the rare blood type. After doing his good deed he just left the building. He had told me when I gave him a lift that he was on the way to the hospital but none of the staff recalled him visiting anyone. It's a mystery why he was heading there and the plot thickens when I tried to track him down to thank him for what he did. For some bizarre reason the forms he filled out for the transfusion and the tests that were done were mislaid.

Nigel didn't meet a mysterious stranger when he was rushed to hospital as a child, but encountered someone he already knew:

Clear choice

At the age of four and a half, I was playing doctors when my cousin gave me a bottle of real tablets. The next thing I recall is waking up in intensive care looking at a monitor. Apparently the doctors had told my parents I would die, as my small body would not be able to withstand the massive overdose. Suffice to say I recall very vividly being surrounded by five beings. I knew them totally and completely. They told me I had a choice. I could come to them or stay and complete a task I had volunteered to do later in life. It's a very long story, actually, to put here, but in short I decided to stay as I knew my parents would be upset.

The experience was very profound and deep. I was told that one day I would know what the task was I had to do. I still don't know what that task is but I do know that I amazed the doctors when I came round and just sat up with no obvious ill effects.

I wrote back to tell Nigel that simply sending in this story and allowing it to be published helps spread the word about healing angels – what higher task could there be?

In some cases angels will manifest their healing to hospital patients not through lights, mysterious visitors, figures shrouded in mist or visions but through unexplained and inexplicable feelings of comfort and warmth during times of trauma. In her email Stephanie described this feeling as like drinking a cup of warm chocolate on a bitterly cold winter's day. Here's her moving story:

Angel in heaven

It has been five years since I held my son, Oliver, in my arms for the first and last time. I remember how very tiny he was and how his little body seemed to fit into the palm of my hands. I remember his last kicks. I remember waking up and knowing he was gone even though he was still inside me. I remember the pain of delivering his lifeless body. I remember the even greater pain when he was taken away from me in hospital and I was given a sedative by the nurse and left on my own to 'rest'.

There was no one there for me. My partner left when I got pregnant and my mother had died five months ago. Oliver was going to be my future and now my future was dead. Without him I felt empty and I wished I was dead myself. I just wanted to disappear, to sleep and never wake up again.

It was when I was lying there feeling hopeless that I felt this tingling sensation at the back of my neck; this feeling grew until I felt this all over my back. I closed my eyes and felt warmth, peace and love. In my mind's eye I could see my mother standing there with Oliver in her arms. I knew he would be safe and well looked after with her. I then felt an angel wrap its wings around me. Sounds daft, but I can only compare the feeling to that of drinking hot chocolate in front of a warm fire on a bitterly cold day.

It was a great experience and very moving. I shall never forget this.

Memories of it helped me pull through the darkest period of my life. Every time I felt low I drew strength from it because I knew that I wasn't alone and that although it may have been Oliver's time to go, it wasn't mine. For Oliver and my mum's sake I needed to live and find my feet and my path in life again.

This happened five years ago and although there have been more tough times I've never sunk as low again. Knowing how ghastly it can be to lose a child I've just completed my training as a midwife and I hope that I can offer comfort and understanding to women like me who don't get to hold their child for long after their delivery. Sometimes I don't say much, I just stay with them and talk to them about their child. Other times I tell them about what happened to me. I try to help and when I can't I pray for angels to visit them as they visited me. Please share my story if you can. It would mean a great deal to me.

I think this next story, sent in by Marie, is intriguing because although it doesn't actually take place in hospital it seems that an angel may actually have led her to hospital:

The painting

I was living a miserable life in Spain with my husband. I like to paint and so one day I took out my canvas and didn't have a clue what I was going to paint. I sort of just went with the flow. The painting took me about thirty minutes to do and I was quite pleased with the end result. I didn't wait for it to dry. I just hung it up straight away on a spare nail I had in the wall just opposite my kitchen. It hung there for a few weeks and I would glance at it now and again.

One day I was feeling really down and wondering what to do with my life with my husband. I looked at my picture and could not believe my eyes. There on the top of the church I had painted was the outline of an angel; the features were just beautiful and the more I looked at this painting the more I could see it was definitely an angel. I thought, how could this be? I could not have painted such a beautiful angel if I tried.

I was very intrigued and wondered if this angel was trying to tell me something. One night as I lay in bed I asked for a sign. I didn't think anything would happen but I was wrong. As I lay there the light I keep on in the hall started to flicker and there were sparkling lights on the ceiling. I was mesmerized and just said over and over to myself, 'Wow!' I knew then and there that there are angels. I also knew in that instant that I shouldn't be in Spain; I should be back in England.

This happened in the middle of last year and by November I had decided to return to England. I am convinced I was led by the angels to do this because when I got back from Spain the first thing I did was go to the doctor's and ask for a check-up for everything, including a mammogram. I'm never usually this careful but as soon as I got back home something told me I must get this done. I wouldn't have done this in Spain, I don't think.

If I hadn't had a check-up I might not be writing this to you. I was found to have the early stages of breast cancer. I was told by the hospital that I was very lucky they caught it in its early stages. I truly believe my guardian angel on my picture led me. I just had an overpowering urge to get here and get to a doctor when I got back to the UK. I doubt I would have gone to one in Spain. The lump was so small even the doctor could not feel it and so it was only picked up with ultrasound.

So many things have happened to me since, too numerous to mention. I am aware now that I am looked after, and what will be will be, and I have so much faith in my angel. The picture is still in Spain as it is too big to bring over on a flight but I will have it shipped over one day. For now I have a photo of it. I am living alone now but don't really feel alone. If I feel down I just ask my angel to take away my sadness and it always seems to work.

Jake's story echoes Marie's in that he also had an overwhelming urge to get to a hospital, for no apparent reason:

The tattoo

I was at the cinema with my girlfriend – watching *Harry Potter and the Half-Blood Prince*. I'm a big fan of the books so was totally absorbed in the film. The trip coincided with my birthday so it was a doubly special day for me. My girlfriend had treated me to the trip and to a meal out. During the day we'd both had some tiny tattoos done on the lower part of our right arms to celebrate our love for each other. I'd chosen to have an angel and my girlfriend had chosen to have a heart tattoo. Why did I choose an angel? I can't answer that. It just spoke to me.

We'd only seen about ten or fifteen minutes of the movie when I began to feel very strange. The tattoo on my arm started to tingle and this feeling of tingling spread throughout my body. I didn't feel hot or sick, I just felt odd. It was like I was about to give an after-dinner speech or something – you know the feeling, kind of excitement mixed with terror. At first I put it down to my excitement that I was watching a much-anticipated movie with my much-loved girlfriend but then – and I know this sounds melodramatic – it suddenly became obvious to me that if I didn't get to a hospital immediately I would die.

I can only describe it in this way. I was perfectly calm and didn't have any dizziness or violent headaches or stomachaches but the feeling that I was about to die was so strong that I turned to my girlfriend and told her that I needed to leave the cinema and get to a hospital. Something in my manner must have convinced her that I wasn't playing games and I was serious.

Fortunately, my cinema isn't too far away from the hospital. My girlfriend didn't say much as we walked there. It took us about thirty minutes. I think she was as confused as I was about everything, but I truly appreciated her belief in me. I know if I'd have gone with anyone else they would have told me I was overreacting and just needed an aspirin or something. As we walked I remember lighting up a cigarette and really savouring it because I knew it would be my last.

When I got to the hospital I remember the resigned look on the receptionist's face when I told her that there was nothing wrong with me right now but if I didn't talk to a doctor soon I was going to die. It was like, here we go, another crazy just walked in. I can't remember much after that because I blacked out.

To cut a long story short, if I hadn't been in hospital that night I would have died. I had a heart attack, which my doctor tells me was probably caused by undiagnosed hypercholesterolemia, which in turn was probably triggered by smoking. Before my heart attack I was a forty-a-day man. My doctor also told me that if I hadn't actually been in hospital paramedics might not have got to me in time to save my life. He also told me the smoking had to go if I wanted to live. Quitting wasn't easy but I've not had a cigarette for three months now. Whenever I feel weak I just look at my angel tattoo – the tattoo that took me to hospital – and the craving goes.

I have often wondered about that night and whether angels were speaking to me or if it was just my intuition. All I know is that I started feeling strange when my angel tattoo started itching and the feelings of discomfort that triggered saved my life.

It's fascinating that Jake believes his angel tattoo was the trigger for his guardian angel to speak to him and save his life, proving once again that just as every person is unique so every angel experience and the manner in which it manifests for them is unique to them.

For many people there is recovery and survival but there's no getting away from the fact that hospitals are also places where people don't recover and may even die. For every miracle healing, for reasons we may never understand, there are countless more cases where suffering doesn't end or life slips away. However, the stories I have collected over the years suggest that even when the angels don't intervene directly they are never far away. Many people have contacted me to say that they saw an angel quietly standing (or is it waiting?) beside the bedside of someone before they passed away, while others have seen 'bright lights'. Often this happens within days and sometimes moments of a person crossing over and, as you'll see in Chapter Six when we return to the subject of angelic encounters before, during and after death, witnesses draw great comfort and strength from these sightings, believing them to be a sign that their loved ones are being looked after and are not alone in their hour of need.

Of course, it isn't just patients and their loved ones who are touched and transformed by angels. Nurses, doctors, care workers and medical staff are as well. As I mentioned at the very start of this chapter, you'd be surprised by just how many doctors there are out there who believe in angels or a subtle yet very real presence that comforts, protects and guides not just their patients but medical professionals themselves too. Bianca's story is compelling because of something she and her doctor seem to have experienced at the same time:

Just breathe

Last year I had to have a delicate operation on my heart. I've had many before, as I was born with a weak heart, but this time I was more scared than before and I prayed that the surgeons would bring me safely in and out of the anaesthetic. I must have breathed in too deeply or something because it took a lot to bring me back to consciousness. I remember catching glimpses of the surgeon and hearing him telling me not to fight things and to breathe. He told me I needed to live. Then I remember seeing this angel step inside the body of the surgeon. For the briefest of instants I could see two bodies as one: the surgeon and the angel inside him, guiding him.

When I came round several hours later I found out that I had nearly died on the operating table and would have done if it hadn't been for the brilliant work of the surgeon and his team. When the surgeon came to visit me I thanked him for what he had done and then the most incredible thing happened. He told me that it had felt to him as though someone was moving his hands. Hearing him speak like this gave me the confidence to tell him what I had seen. I said to him I thought it was my angel. He told me that whatever it was it was absolutely wonderful because he felt as if he had experienced something he just couldn't explain.

If you ever get a chance to talk to a practising medical doctor I'm sure he or she will admit that they either know of or have personal experience of cases which they struggle to explain medically or rationally; or that they have heard of at least one patient with some hopeless condition, as far as modern science is concerned, who suddenly and miraculously recovered. The technical term doctors like to use for cases like this that they simply don't understand is 'spontaneous regression' – in other words, a healing miracle.

CHAPTER 4

Answers from Above

Angels are never too distant to hear you and
if you seek an angel with an open heart you
will always find one.

Author unknown

Continuing the healing-miracle theme, in this chapter we'll explore other ways that angels can manifest their loving presence on earth. None of the people in this chapter saw blinding lights or visions of angels but in each case they are in absolutely no doubt that angels were instructing, guiding, healing and comforting them and that the answers to the questions they asked came from above. Remember, full-blown angel sightings are extremely rare. More common – but, as these stories show, equally as powerful if you allow them to be – are subtle, gentle angel nudges in the form of answers to heartfelt prayers or flashes of profound intuition, premonitions, spectacular coincidences, insightful dreams and other subtle but no less miraculous angel signs.

The angels can help us in any number of ways but they won't be able to bring healing into our lives unless we ask them to. I hesitate to mention the word prayer here as it is so closely bound up with religion and, as I've explained, you don't need to be religious to walk with angels, but one sure-fire way to bring angel healing into your life is to ask them for their help, support and guidance. Anyone, regardless of their belief system, can utter a heartfelt prayer and angels, of course, play an important role here, because they can hear our deepest yearnings and longings and can act as intermediaries between ourselves and a higher power.

If anyone has ever told you that you are in their prayers you may have felt, even for a brief moment, an inexplicable sense of comfort and peace. Experts aren't exactly sure why but it does seem that there is healing power in prayer. Study after study in respected medical journals on various forms of prayer have shown a positive effect on blood pressure, wound healing, heartaches, headaches, depression and anxiety. There have also been reports of people who have recovered from serious or normally fatal illnesses.

A case reported in the *British Medical Journal* in 2002 serves as an example. In the report by Dr Westcott, a GP who describes himself as an atheist, the case is outlined of a non-religious man called Jim suffering from asbestosis which he had acquired as a result of his work as a submarine engineer. Jim was diagnosed with a mesothelioma of the chest wall, a well-known complication of asbestosis, and a malignant tumour. Radiotherapy had little effect and Jim was close to dying.

Jim's wife decided to take her husband to the Greek island of

Kefalonia to spend his final days. While there they visited a monastery. An old nun singled Jim out and asked him what his illness was. She took him to a priest, who prayed for his recovery, and immediately afterwards Jim felt stronger; his recovery continued until his tumour went into remission.

Cases like Jim's suggest that prayer, far from being the last resort, should perhaps be the first resort.

Many medical doctors still remain highly sceptical of healings through unconventional methods such as prayers, laying on of hands, faith in a higher power or pilgrimages to sacred places. The American Medical Association, however, has long recognized the power of faith on the patient's mind as a factor that can positively impact their health and they do not attempt to disprove that healing miracles can and do happen, without any explainable medical cause. Dr Larry Dossey, former chief of staff at Medical City Dallas and author of *Healing Words: The Power of Prayer and the Practice of Medicine*, has taken this one step further by suggesting that the power of prayer to heal is 'one of the best-kept secrets in medical science'.

There are just too many miracle-cure stories around to dismiss the idea that healing powers exist on a spiritual level, even though we may not fully understand them. Indeed, whether they believe in a higher power or not, many doctors and surgeons will tell you that the best kind of medicine is medicine that is carried out with compassion and hope for healing, and, if healing does not occur, hope for the patient to be given the strength to live with his or her illness or disability.

Of course prayers aren't always answered, and they don't always bring the results we hope for, but if we ask the angels to guide us they will be at our side helping to ease our pain and giving us the courage we need to cope. And if we pray on behalf of others this will strengthen the power of the angels to give those in need the inner strength they need. So, if there is someone you care about who is suffering and you don't know how to help or ease their pain, there is something very powerful you can do: you can pray for them.

Sometimes angels will answer our prayers in the form of a dream, or a person appearing in our lives at just the right time to say or do something helpful or meaningful. They can also reply in the form of a still and gentle voice within – call it intuition, or sixth sense or what you will, but angels can manifest their presence in this way through flashes of insight or illumination that give us courage or help us understand or know something with absolutely certainty.

When you get these beautiful 'aha' moments of clarity never dismiss them, because they could save or transform your life – as they did for Debbie, whose story is below:

Higher force

Although I am a science teacher I have always believed in a greater force. I like to think about us all as being part of a lovely energy that we go back to once we die. Being brought up as a Catholic I always felt more open to these ideas. However, when I had my first daughter it was my first real experience of proper contact with 'something'. When I was in the delivery room I actually heard a voice encouraging me and telling me everything was all right and that I would come through it. This voice came from inside my head and although other people, including my husband and nurses, were in the room talking to me it was the only sound I could focus on; it made me feel really calm and protected no matter what. Following the experience I no longer fear dying and truly believe there is an afterlife.

As illustrated by Laura's experience, below, angels don't just hear our formal prayers: they can also hear our silent prayers, those prayers we may have forgotten how to say or not even know we are saying:

Something touched my heart

I'd love to share with you my angel experience because it saved my life.

I can remember from a very young age being in tune with something I couldn't explain. I remember having visions of being awake in my cot at the side of my parent's bed. Things were different then – the style of the wardrobes and even the colour of the walls. When I later told my parents I was there, awake and taking note of these things, they could not believe I could remember such things as I was a very small baby at the time. I remember seeing colours swirling in the room but then other things I could not understand, like jumping figures. Although my parents have always been spiritually aware (both of them) this still amazed them.

Once everyday things started to take over, like school and worries about not having many friends, etc., I began to see and hear next to nothing and after some years wondered if it had been real at all. Then when I was about fifteen I started to go through a very bad time in my life. I'm twenty-one now so this was a good six years ago. I met a boy a few years older on the internet and I very much liked him. When, aged fifteen, I announced we were going to be together, my parents could not contain their horror. After a while I began to feel like they did not love me because they disapproved so much that they stopped talking to me – regardless of whether I was struggling at school or had fallen out with friends.

Eventually, after a year, I decided that the boy wasn't right for me. He told me he was schizophrenic and used to hear the voice of a butler in his head telling him bad things. He also used to say that when we died we went to nothing and I was a fool to believe otherwise. Something about him had, over time, begun to frighten me so I decided to speak to my mum. She agreed that she had for some time seen many frightening characteristics in him and had long feared I was in danger, but she wasn't very kind or sympathetic at the time and simply told me to get rid of him. The atmosphere of not talking to my parents continued despite the revelation that I no longer wanted to be with him and I was lost in depression, believing that no solution had a happy ending.

So there I was at the age of sixteen. I was stuck. I knew I no longer wanted to be with this boy (who loved me intensely and often threatened to take his life if I left him) but I knew that I had been with him for so long that my parents no longer had any regard for me, or so I felt at the time. After weeks of daily tears and circling in my head, feeling that there was no escape, I reached my all-time low.

I remember sitting in the bathroom one evening for what felt like hours. I had been crying again but this time there was no release and I felt numb. It just didn't matter that I was suffering. I sat for a long time and after a while, in my desperation, in my head I shouted at my guardian angel. I told him I could not believe in him because if he was there he had let me down. He had let me suffer so badly that I couldn't feel anything any more. I was born to parents who had come to hate me and had a boyfriend who said he was going to kill himself if I left him.

I told my angel that I would kill myself that night by taking an overdose of tablets, and said if he was real he would stop me and show himself. I said that this was my angel's last chance to show me he was real but that he would have to make this right and make my life worth living again.

I sat for a while in the silence waiting for some explosion and my angel to appear. After feeling and seeing nothing I felt tears run from my eyes, knowing that this was it. Those echoes from my boyfriend rang in my ears and I knew that I would die and go to nothing. Not only that, but there was no angel to save me. Then the most spectacular thing happened.

I had been sitting in the empty bath tub and as I moved forward to get up and out of it something stopped me and made me sit back down. My eyes were closed and, though I saw nothing, someone was there right in front of me holding me in place. Instantly I felt as though someone had touched my heart right through my chest with a love I have felt often since, in my times of need. This love filled the inside of my body, what I know now was my soul. My soul was being re-lit.

At the same time as all this was happening, I heard a voice. It said to me in a loving but authoritative tone, 'It does not matter what happens to you on the outside. Nothing will ever hurt you on the inside.' So at the same time I heard the voice I was feeling this loving and 'charged' feeling consume my whole body. That was a defining moment in my life.

I felt tears run from my eyes, tears not of sadness but of love. I felt like someone had charged my soul but I also felt like someone had given me a huge hug. This was more powerful than anything I had ever felt before in my life. In a second I realized how stupid I had been. I truly believe my guardian angel reached me that day and saved my life. I truly believe I would have taken my own life that day.

Today I attend a spiritualist church and often feel spirit with me. When I'm struggling, I pray to my angels and they help me. But if I have a problem and ask for strength to get through it, I don't pray for the angels to remove it – because everything that happens to us happens for a reason, even pain and suffering. They are with me every time and every time I come out of the other side stronger.

More recently I started to see spirit in a beautiful white light. I don't feel afraid any more. Whenever I am sad I feel the angels there and they fill me with love and make me strong again, just like that day in the bath tub. I can honestly say they have never let me fall again.

Like Laura, many people find that when they leave childhood behind they lose touch with their belief in angels. But even if we lose sight of them or don't think we can hear them any more our angels are never far away. In fact, it is often when we are at our lowest point – when we can see only darkness ahead – that the angels shine their brightest light on us. Episodes of depression, like the darkness before the dawn or the pains of labour, are painful to live through but they also offer incredible opportunities for spiritual growth or rebirth.

Many times in my life I have experienced depression and each time I have pulled through with the help of the angels. I truly believe that in many cases depression is an expression of spiritual hunger, when there is a deep longing to reconnect with the divine within and without us. For some reason we have lost touch with who we truly are, with the belief in angels that is our birthright, and the only way for us to find comfort in the midst of despair is to acknowledge how lost and alone we feel and surrender our hearts and minds to the divine.

It doesn't matter how, where or when or even why you ask for their help; all you need to do is open your heart and invite angel healing in. Whether it is a flash of insight during a time of personal turmoil, as it was for Laura, or just a quiet, simple understanding during a sudden crisis, as it was for Mary, who tells her story below, these things are the voice of your guardian angel calling out to you:

Slow motion

I believe that an angel whispered to me several years ago when I was thrown off the horse I was riding. For some reason my horse just bolted and catapulted me into the air. I was in the air for only a few moments but I can honestly tell you that those few moments felt like slow motion. I'm not medically trained but something inside me told me to relax into the fall. I let my muscles go limp. I didn't fight the fall and landed on my lower back instead of my neck or upper back. I got up without a scratch on me.

The riding school insisted that I visited a doctor to make sure there was no internal injury. My doctor referred me to a back specialist who found a broken vertebrae but otherwise I was all clear. He told me I was extremely lucky. Most bones break when muscles are tense and I must have just fallen in the right way. An inch either way and I might never have walked again. Just thinking about it makes me cry.

A good friend of mine, Paul, sent me his story. Like Mary, he just knew what he had to do:

Where did this feeling come from?

I've never been one to visit the doctor unnecessarily. In fact I have a dislike of hospitals and doctors in general so it came as a huge surprise to me one morning when I woke up with this nagging feeling that I needed to organize a medical. I'm in my mid-thirties and physically active and I felt great so where did this feeling come from?

I ignored it for a week or two but eventually to give myself peace of mind I had a medical. Part of that medical involved a colonoscopy. I don't want to go into the details but a small tumour growth was found. I had it removed immediately. There is no telling what might have happened if I had not listened to my inner voice. In the early stages colon cancer is virtually symptom-free. By the time symptoms appear, such as bleeding and pain, treatment plans have nowhere near the success rate.

For Hazel there isn't a day that passes when she isn't grateful she listened to and acted upon her intuition:

Early night

When we first got married my then husband and I slept in the attic and our son and daughter slept on the floor below us. One night, my kids were about four and five years old at the time, I went to bed earlier than normal. By the time my husband came to bed I was fast asleep.

In the early hours of the morning I woke up feeling unsettled for no reason. I wasn't in any pain; I just felt disturbed. It was not a good feeling. Every time I tried to go back to sleep I woke up again. It was as if I was being prodded awake, not physically but mentally. It was a feeling I can't explain.

Eventually I went down the attic stairs to check on the children. I then walked down to the bottom floor of the house. I should mention here that I'm very scared of the dark but I didn't put on the light because I didn't want to wake anyone up. When I got to the bottom of the stairs I smelled this horrible smell. I opened the door to the dining room and even though it was pitch dark, I soon realized that the smell was gas. I opened the kitchen door and could hear the cooker hissing while gas poured out of it.

It turned out that my husband had moved his lunch bag before going to bed and the strap had hooked around the control knob. Inadvertently he had managed to turn on the stove as he walked away.

I have never stopped wondering if it was coincidence that I woke up but it really felt as if someone was not allowing me to sleep and something told me to go downstairs. The house was full of gas when I opened the kitchen door. If I had turned on the lights there could have been an explosion. I'm scared of the dark so why didn't I turn on the lights? My children were fast asleep so really it would not have woken them up.

What if I hadn't woken up that night? My children were nearer the gas source than my husband and me and they would have been in deadly danger. I would love to know if this was the work of my guardian angel or maybe my children's guardian angel. I suspect I will never know but I also suspect there was someone looking out for me that night.

Sometimes it is not a voice that we hear but, as Gina describes, a 'feeling' that overtakes us:

The right path

It was late in the night and I was walking home from hospital. My husband had been involved in a car crash and it was touch and go so my thoughts were all about him. I took the quickest route I could home. I was anxious to be with my kids. Looking back, this was not a sensible decision because it was not the safest route to take. As I was walking I heard these footsteps shuffling behind me. I saw a couple of guys walking up to me. Something about them made me feel uneasy so I started to run. Things got worse when I heard that they were running too.

Then out of the blue I felt a presence. It was like the feeling you get when you're young and you cuddle up to your mum and suck your thumb. I felt completely safe, like something was wrapping its arms around me. It was a feeling of comfort and strength I had not felt before. I stopped running and stood still, drinking it all in. While I was standing still I watched the two guys run past me. They looked really scared of me. Can you believe that? They were scared of me. I'm only just over five feet and a hundred pounds and they looked big and tough. I know something extraordinary happened to me that night.

Cynthia's story, detailed below, shows that sometimes the still, quiet voice we hear within can transform into the voice of someone else:

Definitely there

In 2002 I was working as a carer for the elderly. For four nights in a row I could smell this smoky smell that lingered beside me; everywhere I turned it was there. I also had what could only be described as a bad chest infection.

One night while I was at work the chest pains were so bad I had to come home, have a bath and go to bed. I thought I was asleep but I could plainly hear my dad's voice – he passed away with a heart attack in 1988 – saying I was only fifty-two and needed to get sorted. I was frightened and jumped out of bed. I told my partner and he said I must have been dreaming. I don't think I was, though.

It happened again the next night and on the Saturday morning I had a heart attack. I survived it but needed coronary stents fitted so I was booked in to have this operation a few months later. Things took another turn and I needed the stents put in sooner rather than later. I was admitted on 8 December (the anniversary of my dad's passing) and had the operation on 12 December (the anniversary of my dad's burial). I have no doubt that my guardian angel was definitely there.

I'm often asked how you can tell if it is fear or your angel speaking to you and my answer is always the same. In the case of fear there will be a lot of words and noise going around in your head. Your guardian angel speaking through your intuition is a lot quieter. When you know something you just know it without a lot of words to explain it, even if it is illogical. When you are afraid there are long, drawn-out explanations in your head – anything but a quiet knowing of the truth.

The voice of your guardian angel is also much gentler than fear. If the thoughts in your head are filled with anxiety, guilt and judgement they are not from the world of spirit. Your angel tends to be warm, comforting, kind and non-judgemental. Fear tends to paralyse you so you can't make any decisions or move forward; your angel guides you in the right direction. If the voice in your head says you are a loser, you always quit, you can't do what it takes, it isn't your angel speaking. Your angel will tell you that something doesn't feel right, that this isn't the right thing for you, that it is better to change direction or move on and find what is best for you. There may be no words at all, just a gut feeling that it is time to make a change or that you need to say or do something.

Never underestimate the power of the still, quiet voice of your inner angel that speaks within you because, as Lucy's story illustrates, it could prove to be absolutely crucial:

Tuning in

I never thought I was psychic but after what happened last week I think I might be. I was in my house getting supper ready for the kids when I had this overpowering feeling something was wrong with my friend. I phoned her up and she sounded fine on the other end of the phone. When I asked her if she was okay she just laughed and told me not to worry. She was being treated to a candlelit meal by her boyfriend.

The phone call still didn't give me peace of mind so I handed supper duties over to my husband and jumped into my car. My hands shook at the steering wheel. It took about twenty minutes for me to get to my friend's house – it was a Friday night and traffic was bad – and when I got there I leaped out of my car and banged on the door. I knew she was in because the light was on and she had told me she was having supper with her boyfriend. There was no answer and then I heard shouting coming from upstairs. I called out to her and saw her run to the window and mouth the word help. I didn't hesitate: I phoned the police.

Turns out this boyfriend of hers – I never liked him much – had viciously attacked her. There were bruises on her face and the second and third fingers of her hands were broken. He had smashed her hands with the piano cover when she was practising before dinner because he didn't like what she was playing. I had tuned into her fear.

Ryan sent me this next story. Like Lucy, he was also able to tune into the feelings of someone he cared about:

Strange feelings

I was doing my morning rounds – I'm a postal worker – when I got this strange feeling. I just knew that something was wrong with my sister. I can't explain it. I was convinced that she needed me. I rang her mobile and there was no answer. I called the hairdresser's where she works and they asked me if she was ill, because she was late for work.

Immediately I knew something was very wrong. My sister has hearing and vision problems and lives alone and I was worried that she might have fallen or something. When I got to her house I heard her dog barking in the garden. She only let him out when she was at home so I started to panic.

I rang on the doorbell. There was no answer. I had to smash a window to get in and my heart nearly stopped when I saw her at the bottom of the stairs. She was lying on her stomach. I rushed over and turned her over. There was a gash on the top of her head. I was right. She had fallen down the stairs. I tried to wake her up but she was far away.

I called for the ambulance. They arrived a horrible fifteen minutes later. In that time I listened to all the advice the emergency helpline gave me. I prayed for my sister to live. For the next seven days I barely left her side. At one point doctors were worried about brain damage but she pulled through.

Doctors have told me that if I hadn't been there my sister might have died. I didn't tell them that if a voice hadn't told me that my sister needed me I might not have been there. The voice was clearly telling me to go to her.

The miracles don't stop there. After the blow to her head from the fall my sister's vision improved. It's not perfect but she can see much more clearly than before. My sister's doctors can't explain why her sight has improved. Like me, they call it a miracle.

In both the above stories angels spoke to the person involved through their loving concern for someone other than themselves. Empathy – connecting to others by imagining or sensing what things look or feel like for them – is one of the most powerful human emotions. It is also the first step to psychic awareness. So if you don't think you are psychic, but you find that people open up to you easily because you always sense what they are feeling, or that your eyes fill with tears when you watch weepy movies, or when you hear about or witness the suffering of others, you have the natural gift of empathy and it is through that gift that your guardian angel will call out to you. Everybody is born with the gift of empathy and all you need to do to unlock its powers is to trust it.

The first awareness you may have of your angel speaking within you is through feelings. Feelings are the language of your angels. Have you ever felt alone when you were in a group of people? Or angry or sad when you don't know why? You don't need to act on these feelings; you just need to observe them and see what you can learn from them because your angel may be trying to tell you something. Your job is simply to listen, as Charlotte did:

First aid

While on holiday in Majorca I booked a day trip at the market with a coach party. Before I got on the coach I called at the shop for a newspaper, where something happened to me that I couldn't understand. For some unknown reason I bought medical wipes, lint, small scissors and a role of plasters. It felt like someone was telling me to do this.

Later when I was walking through the market I heard someone screaming. I turned around and saw an old lady with blood pouring from her leg. I sat on a wall and tended to her injury and a stallholder gave her a sip of brandy for the shock. I walked on and thanked the angel on my shoulder for using me to help this lady.

Donna also followed her instincts:

One last farewell

One of my friends, Sonia, threw this party back in 2001. She told everyone that she was going to start a new life abroad and that this was her last farewell. Dozens of people turned up and there was an atmosphere of excitement and fun as we all admired Sonia's courage. About halfway through the party I started to feel really sad whenever I chatted to Sonia. She seemed happy enough but the more I looked at her the more I saw this white light wrapping around her shoulders. I don't know much about these things but it could have been her aura. Other people didn't seem to notice it so I wondered if I had been drinking too much.

As the party wore on I got more and more depressed. I put it down to Sonia leaving but we hadn't been such close friends. The guy who gave me a lift to the party and wasn't drinking was one of the last to leave so I had to hang around longer than I would normally have. When the time came for us to say our last goodbyes I wondered whether I should tell Sonia about what I saw and felt. She might think I was nuts or something. Anyway, perhaps it was the drink talking or something much more powerful but I ended up blurting out that she shouldn't feel sad or scared about starting a new life abroad because all through the party I had seen an angel on her shoulder.

Sonia gulped and then started to cry. I hadn't been prepared for that reaction at all so I was at a loss for words. I just patted her on the shoulder and apologized for upsetting her. She shook her head and told me that this party was indeed a farewell party but not the kind everyone thought it was. Ever since her marriage had broken down last year and she had been diagnosed with diabetes she had lost the will and energy to live and had planned to take her life as soon as the last guest had left. She had already written a letter to her family telling them that she didn't want a funeral because her farewell party had been the best send-off anyone could wish for. She also told me that she had begged for a sign that the angels were watching over her and now I had given her hope again. She knew she wasn't alone.

After such an emotional encounter Sonia and I stayed in touch for several years. We don't talk to each other as much as we used to now I'm married and raising my family, but last thing I heard she had retrained as a teacher and was working in a busy comprehensive school. The kids loved her, apparently, and she loved her job.

Empathy for others, understanding and tuning into their spirits, can have the same healing and strengthening power as prayer. It has this strength because whenever there is love and connection between people the power of the angels to send their love and healing increases.

A lovely lady, whom I will call Patience here because the contents of the email are so personal, sent me this inspiring story about the unbreakable bond of love and connection that exists between her, her father and her son:

Always beside me

My father died in January 2003 and I was devastated, as we were very close. In September 2004 I got up the day before my son Martin's eighteenth birthday and could feel my dad very close to me. It was very strange. He had given me a necklace four years before with footprints on it and a line from the 'Footprints in the Sand' poem engraved on the back; I just had to put it on. I can't explain how or why but I just knew something was wrong.

My husband had bought my son a motorbike a few weeks previously for his birthday, and I wasn't very pleased about it. Anyway his birthday came and went, but on the following Tuesday on my way home from work my husband phoned me to say that Martin had had an accident. I was beside myself trying to get home but the traffic was awful and everyone was ringing me and texting me to find out where I was. Eventually I was about two miles from home when my tyre went flat. I pulled into the garage and just knew that Martin was dead. I could feel my dad close to me.

Anyway, to cut a long story short, four months later my husband left me. I tried to get on with my life but I was so unhappy and lonely. I took an overdose and ended up on a mental-health ward. During my time there I swear that on a number of occasions someone sat on my bed and gave me a hug, but I could not see anyone. My husband came to the hospital every day and promised my doctors and nurses he would look after me and bring me back to Ireland to live. Of course he changed his mind when I came out of the hospital, and left me alone again. I went to a friend's house for Christmas and had a good time there but something was driving me to return to Ireland. I booked a flight to Ireland and in a week I found a lovely house in the country, and I am so sure my dad found this house for me, absolutely sure of it; it felt like I had come home.

Three weeks later I travelled from the UK to begin my new life in Ireland. It was the week of the bad storms. The weather was dreadful but I could sense my son in the car with me and I felt completely calm and safe. It took me three days, driving without sleep, and I only got rest on the ferry, which was a bumpy ride because of the storm. Since then I have had numerous things happen with my son and my dad. I know without a doubt that they are taking care of me and giving me strength every day to carry on.

Writing about those bad years I have left an awful lot of things out, but the last two years I have been in Ireland have been so good to me and I have changed beyond belief. I am stronger and more confident than I have ever been in my life. I never thought that I would be happy to live alone in the country but then I never really feel alone. Every day I feel Dad and Martin around me. They have made me what I am today and I love them so much.

Patience is in no doubt that the bond of love she has with her father and son cannot be broken by death. With them always by her side she never feels alone.

As we've seen, angels can speak to you through your intuition and your feelings. All you need to do is find a still place within you so you can tune into them. When there is a strong emotional bond between two people, like that which exists between parent and child, intuition tends to be at its most powerful because, as mentioned before, love is the language that angels speak and angels cluster when the bonds of love are at their strongest.

Everyone – yes, everyone – is born with intuition and we have all had experiences of it, even if we don't think we have. Think about it. Have you ever thought of someone you haven't seen for a while and then the phone rings and it is them? Have you ever said something and the person you are talking to says they were thinking exactly the same thing?

Throughout history many of the world's greatest artists, leaders and achievers have based their decisions on intuition – or hunches, insights, visions, sixth sense, gut feeling, which are just other names for it. What all these people have been doing is communicating with the angel inside themselves. They have listened to their inner angel and allowed it to give them wings. But it isn't just high achievers who are capable of being extraordinary. We are all capable of greatness if we understand that the invisible guardian angel inside us is our inspiration and our gift. And if we all listened to the voice of that inner angel more often we would become more like angels ourselves and so make earth more like heaven.

Children are born with their intuition highly developed. Recognizing and responding to it is something they do instinctively and naturally because they are fresh from heaven. Watching children listen to their inner angel can encourage us to look for our own. If you ever need a shot in the arm to believe in angels, talk to children.

I have often felt that children are far closer to the angels than we adults are. They seem far more ready to share joy freely and to give love unconditionally to others. They seem to easily know how to celebrate life, laugh, smile, and embrace delight just as those angels want us to do. Nothing brought this point home to my heart more clearly than this story sent to me by Karen about her daughter, Katy:

Lady in the park

We were in the park and I was getting a bit bored watching my daughter Katy swing backwards and forwards on the swing. We'd been there for more than half an hour and I wanted to get home. I had a lot to do that evening. Katy begged me to let her stay for just five more minutes and when these five minutes turned into twenty minutes I started to get really cross. It was time to get firm so I grabbed her by the hand and started to pull her away. It was then that she said something really strange.

'I can't go till I've seen the lady.'

'What lady?' I asked.

'I dunno,' she replied, 'but I need to see her.'

There was no one in the playground. It was close to six o'clock now so I thought Katy was just using more delaying tactics. I told her to stop being so selfish and that we were going.

She struggled a bit but eventually I got my way and we left the playground. We had just shut the gate behind us when Katy wriggled her hand out of mine and ran towards this lady who was leaning against a tree with a cigarette in her hand. She then gave this lady a high-five. I was gobsmacked. This wasn't like her: she was bossy with me but very shy with strangers. She still hadn't said a word to her second-grade teacher.

I ran up to the woman and started to apologize for my daughter's peculiar behaviour but she interrupted me and told me with tears in her eyes that her own grown-up daughter had died just a week ago. She had come to the park today because it brought back memories of when she used to take her daughter there years ago. She then went on to say that she had felt so alone and wasn't sensing her daughter around her but Katy had changed all that. She was convinced that Katy coming up to her like this was a sign from her daughter that she was still close. Because of my Katy she believed that there was still love in the world.

There does indeed seem to be a special closeness between angels and children. Children are able to listen to the voice of their angel because grown-up fear, doubt, scepticism and 'rules' about what is or is not appropriate behaviour just aren't there. Unfortunately, this innate ability to hear the voice of their inner angel declines with age but it doesn't have to fade. We can all rediscover, nurture and cherish the child within.

The child within is the child you once were, the child who needed to be loved, cared for and nurtured. It is still within you however old you are. It is the part of you that is loving, receptive, curious, playful, emotional and spontaneous, adventurous, enthusiastic and passionate, but it is also the part most in need of comfort and guidance. Many of us lose touch with our inner child as we grow older but it stays with us all our lives. At heart we are all children searching for meaning in life and it is through our inner child that the angels connect with us. In other words, with unconditional love, trust in the miraculous and an open mind, anyone, whether they are eight or eighty, can hear, see or sense the nearness of their guardian angel. Anyone can stay young in spirit and reclaim that special bond with heaven, a bond that is our birthright.

Over the years I've heard countless stories about children who can hear and see angels. I love how easily children accept and don't question what they see. When I do informal surveys and ask them to tell me about angels they talk in such a factual way. To children it is just simple and obvious that angels are real. Yes, you could dismiss everything as imagination, but the amazing thing about children is their ability to suspend disbelief and it is this ability that makes them more receptive to angel visitations.

From the very first spark of life we are all blessed with a guardian angel and if we follow our intuition – the voice of our angel – we can find fulfilment and happiness. Many of us give in to negative emotions and when this happens it is easy to stop listening to our intuition. But, when we sit calmly and take the time to listen to the answers within, our guardian angel is always there to help and guide us make decisions, influencing us through hunches, dreams, coincidences and signs.

Because we have free will angels can't help and guide us if we are not willing to open our minds and believe in the impossible in the way that a child can. Therefore, encouraging our children to trust what they see, hear and feel – even when we can't see, hear or feel it ourselves – is crucial. Today our children are getting terrible messages about the world we live in. The news is filled with stories of violence, hatred and injustice. Children everywhere need to learn more about angels and the message of love they bring. They need to learn, as we all do, to listen to the answers that come from both above and within. We may not be able to find answers to all the questions that distress us but belief in angels can give us all the sense of certainty and comfort we crave.

Stories about children and angels could fill a book in themselves. I'm just drawing your attention to them here because I believe children have so much to teach us about listening to and trusting our intuition and the answers that come from within.

Another common but frequently neglected or dismissed way for angels to communicate their love and healing from within is through our dreams. Dreams are often forgotten on waking but if you pay attention to them, as Sara did in her story, below, they can be life-changing or even life-saving:

She's stuck

I had quite a vivid angel dream in 2005. I was going through a bit of a tough time. I was twenty-five and had just moved back home. I didn't know where my life was going; I was heartbroken because of the end of a long-term relationship and I was jobless.

I went to bed one night in my attic bedroom, which had a skylight window. I could lie in bed and see the stars most nights, but this particular night had a full moon. I stood on my bed and peeked out the window at the moon before I got into bed. When I lay in bed I couldn't see the moon, as it was low in the sky. I drifted off to sleep.

In my dream I became aware of a bright light. I told myself it was the full moon shining through the window. In fact, this light couldn't have been the moon, because it moved across the night sky and seemed to give off heat. All I know is that I was in a half-awake, half-asleep state. I physically opened my eyes and saw a bright warm light. I smiled and shut my eyes. Then all of a sudden I was in a white room, on a white bed, surrounded by beings in white. I don't recall a great deal of detail about how they looked, just that they were tall beings in white. The atmosphere was calm. I could hear the beings talking. They spoke quite candidly about me. They were having a good old chat. The only thing I remember from their conversation is when one of them said, 'Looks like she's stuck.' Hardly prophetic, but frank.

Then these beings started to heal me. They laid their hands on me and moved my arms and turned my body as if going over every inch of me. I briefly woke up and laughed in my bed because my arm was up in the air and it gently fell to the bed as if being moved. Whatever was happening, whatever they were doing, felt so good. I kept falling asleep and waking up mid-move, because I was being moved. I was still aware of this bright light all the while shining through the window.

At one point when I woke up, I turned over on to my side because that's what they were telling me to do; they were still working on me, and I just smiled and said 'thank you' out loud. When I woke up the next morning I felt renewed. My life didn't change dramatically overnight, but a couple of months later I got a job in Japan, where I lived for a year before returning to England where I met and fell in love with my husband. I now have two children and I am very happy!

Like Sara, Kathy also had a dream that comforted and reassured her:

Doing the right thing

My father died of throat and stomach cancer on 3 August 2007. I wasn't sure if this is what he wanted but I had him cremated because he didn't make his wishes known. Two months ago he came to me in a dream and he looked so well and happy. In my dream he told me that he was very pleased with and proud of me for the lovely funeral I had arranged for him. I can't remember everything he said but we had a lovely chat and again he told me that he had a great send-off. He held my hand and then I woke up.

My friend often tells me that dreams don't mean anything but I just know this dream was different.

Dreams often don't seem to make sense so many people may tell you that they are meaningless and that you should ignore them, as they did in Kathy's case, but this would be a terrible waste. Dreams can be a valuable tool for helping you sort out problems and issues in your daily lives if you become familiar with the symbolic language in which they speak. For example, someone dying in a dream doesn't mean they are actually going to die. It simply means that one phase in your life is ending and another is beginning.

Dreams are also a safe and comforting medium for angels and spirits of departed loved ones to communicate to us; but I'm not talking here about the great majority of dreams we have, which need to be interpreted because they don't make sense, nor about dreams that are soon forgotten after waking. I'm talking here about dreams that are so lucid, so memorable and so obviously 'out of this world' that taking them literally is the only option. The dream I had of my father soon after he died is a good example because it was so intense and I can never forget it. I call this kind of dream a night vision.

Mandi may well have had a night vision during her childhood. She wrote to tell me about a dream she had that many years later still lingers and stays fresh in her mind:

He's gone

When I was nine my grandfather was dying of cancer. At the time I was not told he was dying, just that he was ill. One night I dreamed he had died and I saw who was with him, where everyone was in the house and what they were doing at the time. It was as if I had taken the roof off the house in my dream and was watching from above. I woke up when I heard my aunt say gently, 'He's gone.'

In the morning I asked my mum if Granddad was okay and she said he had slept well and had a good night. I felt horrible that I had dreamed about him dying. The following night my mum and dad went to help with Granddad, as they had done for weeks now. I was happy because I was allowed to stay up later than normal.

A few hours later my aunt came in. I just knew by looking at her that Granddad had died. I felt very peaceful and calm, even though I had loved Granddad very much. She asked me if Mum had phoned, but she hadn't. My sisters were very upset and my aunt took care of them. She didn't ask me how I knew that Granddad had died.

I never mentioned my dream until years later when my aunt and Mum were discussing his death. They asked me how I had known and I told them of my dream. I could still remember it clearly all that time later. Mum was shocked because everything had happened the night my Granddad died exactly as I had dreamed it.

If you aren't sure if you have had a dream or a night vision that involved a visitation from an angel or a lost loved one, the single most important deciding factor is that the dream will be brilliantly vivid and impossible to forget. You have no idea why or how but you know what you experienced was more than a dream because it stays fresh forever in your mind.

In addition to night visions, another brilliantly vivid and unforgettable medium for angels to communicate to us is premonitions, or flash forwards into the future. Sometimes these premonitions manifest in dream form. The terrorist atrocities of 11 September 2001 were preceded by a slew of dream premonitions. A week before the attack, one North Carolina mother dreamed about spinning into blackness and heard a man's voice repeating '2,830, 2,830' – the final tally of victims. The woman cancelled tickets the family had to fly to Disneyland on 11 September, despite protestations from her husband that she was overreacting. When news emerged of the planes flying into New York's Twin Towers the woman wondered if she had somehow had a sixth sense about flying that day.

Sadly, dream premonitions are often too vague and unspecific to avert disaster but in some instances they are specific enough to allow the dreamer enough time to alter the course of the disaster. Here's Hilary's story:

Flash forward

It was a stormy night and I'd gone to bed early. The kids were asleep in their rooms and I lay there listening to the wind and rain beating against the windows. I must have drifted off to sleep because I remember this vivid dream. In my dream I was standing in my daughter's bedroom and the window had smashed. My daughter wasn't in her bed and there was glass all over it. The alarm on her Disney clock was ringing. I looked at it and it read three thirty-two.

I woke with a start and looked at my alarm clock. It was ten past one in the morning. The dream had shaken me up a bit so I crept into my daughter's bedroom. She was curled up with her tiger and looked very peaceful. Her night light was still on so I bent down to switch it off. As I did I heard the wind rattling against her window. With the image of my dream still fresh in my mind I picked her up and took her back to bed with me. I did the same with my son.

With my children snuggled up beside me I settled down to sleep but a few hours later I was woken up by this almighty crash coming from my daughter's bedroom. The violence of the storm had indeed smashed her window right in. There was this huge triangle-shaped piece of glass and it had embedded itself right into her pillow. I shudder to think what might have happened if I hadn't taken her into bed with me. I'd been given a warning. I'd had a kind of flash forward.

The next morning when I came to the room to tidy up I noticed that my daughter's Disney clock had been flung on the floor. It was broken and the time on the clock read three thirty-two, just as my dream had indicated it would.

And sometimes a person can experience a flash forward when they are awake. Nicky still can't believe what happened to her two years ago:

See your father

One day I was heading home from my studio when I got this sudden urge to see my father. I had this image in my head of him lying on the floor having a fit. The feeling was so prominent that I immediately turned my car around and went to see him even though I had not called him or planned to visit him that day.

When I got to my father's flat he was absolutely fine. I thought I was going crazy. He was so happy to see me, though, that I decided to make an evening of it. We chatted and played a game of chess before eating a simple supper of fish and chips. Then just as I was about to leave my father turned pale and seemed to crumble in a heap on the floor. I immediately called for an ambulance and mercifully they were able to revive him. He went on to live for three more years before passing away peacefully in his sleep.

But this sixth sense is not confined to humans. There are count-less examples of apparent premonitions among animals. Just before the Boxing Day tsunami of 2004, flamingos on India's southern coast fled, monkeys at Sri Lanka's Yala National Park stopped accepting bananas from tourists and elephants began to trumpet. I think you'll find this story sent to me by Shirley as fas-cinating as I did:

Change of mind

Almost every morning I have a familiar routine. I get up the same time, get dressed and leave my flat in King's Cross at the same time. I grab a Starbucks and then a paper and then jump on to the tube and, if the tubes are running on time, I arrive at work around the same time.

One morning my clockwork routine broke down because my nor-mally independent and well-behaved cat changed my mind. I fed him as usual and got ready for work but when I put my coat on and grabbed my bag he started meowing. He rarely meows and only purrs at night when we cuddle on the sofa so this really surprised me. As I said, he isn't really an attention-seeking cat during the day, so my first thought was that he wasn't well.

I love my cat so I dropped my bag and picked him up. I checked him all over and there didn't seem to be any sign of pain or discomfort or a wound or anything. He still wouldn't stop wailing so I sent a text to my PA saying that I'd be half an hour later this morning. Perhaps Snoops just felt lonely, so I gave him a lengthy cuddle until he was sleepy and put him in his basket. He was out of the basket as fast as I put him in and wide awake again. What was going on?

Finally, about thirty minutes later, I was able to get out of the door. It wasn't easy, as Snoops is an indoor cat and he was trying to bolt out of the door – again something he has never done. He only tries to escape when I get the Hoover out.

Running behind schedule, I didn't have time for my coffee and paper and started to jog towards the tube station. When I got close I was almost knocked over by this crowd of people rushing up the stairs. There was a sense of panic in the air and there was lots of crying, shouting and screaming. It was the panic and confusion caused by the 7/7 London bombings on the Underground, the Underground that I could well have been on had my cat not made me late that morning. I still get tearful and anxious when I think how close I had been to death or injury that day.

What makes this story so remarkable is that this cat's behaviour can't be explained by a cat's superior sense of hearing or smell or sensitivity to changes in the environment because this was a man-made disaster, not a natural one. On that morning Shirley followed her heart and not her watch and this may just have saved her life.

Sandra is similarly convinced an angel was protecting her:

The white owl

I would like to tell you about something that happened to my husband and me when we were in Australia. We were travelling around and my brother, who lives there, warned us to be very careful when we drove after dark as accidents involving kangaroos were common in the area we were visiting. We often saw dead kangaroos at the side of the road, which I found very distressing.

One evening we were driving through a lonely heavily wooded area and I was so afraid of hitting one of these poor creatures that I prayed it wouldn't happen. Just then ahead of us a huge white owl gently floated down on to the road. We had plenty of time to stop. It sat in the middle of the road with its head turned to the direction we were travelling. We sat transfixed for a few minutes then the owl turned its head, looked at us and took off into the night.

I'm convinced it was stopping us from hitting a kangaroo. Our journey was easy after that and I didn't feel anxious any more. I shall never forget it.

I'd like to talk more here about intuition and sixth sense, both human and animal, but once again that will have to wait until another book. It's time to move on now to another way that angels can send answers from above and that is through the magic of coincidences or synchronicity.

Synchronicity

Sometimes angels answer our prayers in a way that sceptics like to describe as 'just coincidence', but when it happens to you it always feels so much more than that. We've all experienced it – a friend calls when you are thinking about them, someone you get on very well with shares the same birthday as you, a book falls off the shelf, you open it and the words you read hit you between the eyes or you find yourself in just the right place at just the right time. Some coincidences are small, but others really grab our attention and have the potential to change lives. Are these coincidences or answers from above?

What I have read and seen leaves me in no doubt that startling coincidences give witness to power from a higher source. If we close our minds it is easy to dismiss a coincidence as random chance. A song that speaks to our heart just happened to be playing on the radio at a time we needed to hear it most, a white feather that just happened to float in front of our noses out of nowhere, and so on. If, however, we can stop thinking and questioning and simply open ourselves to the idea that perhaps something wonderful is working with us our lives can be transformed.

In *The Celestine Prophecy*, a surprise bestseller published a few years ago, the author, James Redfield, suggested that there is a pattern or guidance of people and the world towards a higher purpose and that the first way to become conscious of this movement forward is to tap into the coincidences in our lives. I don't agree with every one of the insights in Redfield's book but I do agree that coincidences can be signs from our angels that show us the way to go next. Again and again they give us the feeling that angels are watching over us; and focusing more intensely on the deeper meaning of coincidences in our lives can be a first step towards inviting angelic guidance into our lives.

All I have experienced, heard, read and seen leads me to believe that in coincidences the angels are calling out to us. Looking back I can see how much coincidence has played a part in shaping my life. I may not have been able to see it at the time but every person I have met, every experience I have ever had, even those that made me unhappy at the time, has brought me to the place I am today. The place I feel I am meant to be. Just think about your life. What situations just seemed to work out? Think about the people in life. What amazing coincidences brought you all together? What incredible coincidences are waiting out there for you to discover them?

Again and again I have found that when we are on the right path, when we are doing what we are meant to be doing, the number of wonderful coincidences we experience increases; opportunities present themselves and progress becomes easier. When I first agreed to write about angels, after many years as a diet and health author, doors suddenly began to open. Out of the blue I was asked to write more angel books, one of which entered the top ten on the *Sunday Times* bestsellers list. Then newspapers and magazines got in touch and the number of emails and letters sent to me about angelic encounters snowballed. There were many more signs from my angels. In the very first week I started writing I kept finding white feathers on the ground and after that not a day passed when I did not see coins and pick them up. They became my pennies from heaven.

Once you start asking for signs and then paying attention to coincidences, trusting them, listening to them and expressing gratitude for them, you will find that they begin to happen more often. Trust, open-mindedness and feelings of gratitude create an awesome power in the spirit world that can invite spectacular coincidences into your life. When you need support to take you forward in life, that support will come.

★

Like many people who have been inspired, comforted or saved by the miracle of coincidence, Helen is in no doubt that a higher power is looking out for her:

Much more than that

I was driving on a major road on my way to work when for some reason, even though I was being very patient that day, this little voice kept telling me to go in the other lane and go faster. And as soon as I was in the other lane a huge section of gypsum plasterboard flew out of the pickup truck I had been behind and smashed on the road where my car would have been. Well, you can call it coincidence but I think it was much more than that.

This incredible story was told to Pamela by her mum:

The doorbell

My mum told me this story many times. It happened back in 1976, when my eldest brother would have been three years old, my other brother just a small baby and I was perhaps waiting in the spirit world to be conceived.

At the time my dad worked nightshifts six days a week. One night while my dad was at work, in the very early hours of the morning (it was more than thirty years ago now, so Mum cannot be certain of the exact time) the doorbell started ringing, not just a light ring but held in for a few seconds. My mum jumped up, thinking perhaps my dad had got off shift early and for some reason had no key. The street we grew up in was very quiet, full of young families and in the seventies still had the community spirit that seems to have faded somewhat over the years.

Anyway, Mum explained that she didn't even give it a second thought beyond it being my dad so she went downstairs and opened the door; but there was no one there. My dad's car wasn't there and there was no one to be seen and no noise to be heard. She went back upstairs thinking it was strange but she was tired and put her head back on the pillow. The doorbell went again. This time she ran downstairs, opened the door as quick as she could and again . . . No one to be seen or heard. Slightly alarmed, she locked the door this time, checked around the house and made her way back upstairs again.

On passing my brother's bedroom door, which was slightly ajar, Mum noticed a faint smell of something plastic burning. She went in the room and the smell was so strong she turned the light on. Then she could actually see signs of smouldering coming from the small bed my brother lay on sound asleep. She gently woke him and picked him up; his pyjamas were red hot. She put him into her room out of harm's way. The electric blanket had blown and started to actually melt. She pulled everything she could touch off the bed and within seconds the material caught fire.

Mum firmly believes that had she not been woken up by the doorbell my brother could have died.

Pamela's story could, of course, once again be explained away as pure coincidence. Perhaps there were kids playing pranks that night? Perhaps the doorbell was defective and just happened to go off at the right time? But Pamela firmly believes that there is someone looking out for her family. She has yet to meet or see an angel but she knows they are with her.

A doorbell also features in this next intriguing story, sent to me by Harriet:

Mr Right?

For most of the last ten years I worried myself sick that my beautiful and clever daughter, Beth, wouldn't settle down. She had a lot of boyfriends but none of them really understood her. She couldn't find someone she wanted to spend the rest of her life with. She wanted someone intelligent and funny who loved the arts and travel, like she did, and wasn't going to settle for anyone just for the sake of it. Beth's an only child and there was just me and her when she was growing up. We are so close but I'm not going to be around forever and I wanted to know she was happy.

For several years, during her late twenties and early thirties, I made it clear to Beth that I would feel much happier if she were married, but eventually I came to terms with the idea that this might not happen. I let go of my dreams for her and watched her create her own. I saw her build a successful career and earn more money than I could ever have dreamed of. I saw her travel the world. I saw her laugh. I saw her cry. I saw her live the life I wanted to live.

I thought Beth was happy but when she hit forty-four she phoned me up one Sunday afternoon in tears. She confessed to me that she was lonely. All her friends had married and at work all her colleagues would ask her about her love life, or lack of it. It was wearing her down. I reminded her about all her friends who had ended up

125

divorced or who were in dull and lifeless marriages, and about women who knew their husbands were being unfaithful but put up with it. I told her that she still had her freedom and she could still do just about anything she wanted, including marriage and kids if that was what she wanted. I really meant every word I was saying. I couldn't believe how much I had changed over the years. The old marriage-minded me would simply not have been able to console her but I had changed.

I asked Beth if she would like me to come round and spend the evening with her. Beth said she would like that very much. She asked me to ring the buzzer of her flat four times so she knew it was me. She couldn't face seeing any of her friends because her face was swollen and red with crying.

I stopped at a couple of shops to buy some comfort food and arrived at Beth's about an hour later. When I arrived she told me that the strangest thing had happened. About thirty minutes after our phone call the doorbell had rung four times. She had gone down expecting it to be me but it wasn't. It was a guy visiting someone else in her block of flats and he had pressed the wrong bell by accident. The guy looked familiar and it turned out that they had been in the same form at school thirty years ago.

The story doesn't end here. My daughter has been dating this guy for ten months now and he really seems to be perfect for her. I've never seen her so happy and when my daughter is happy I'm happy. I don't know if marriage is on the cards but it is a possibility. Even if it isn't, though, I have a good feeling about this guy and I think he will be around a long time. They have so much in common.

When you think about all the coincidences that brought Beth and her boyfriend together it really makes me think that nothing we do, say or think is ever random.

Rebecca is also convinced that angels are never far away and that the miraculous things that have happened to her are not coincidental:

No explanation

I often feel I have a guardian angel watching over me as I suffered nine consecutive miscarriages in three years. There was no medical explanation for them, which was one of the hardest things to deal with.

In November 2005 I fell pregnant for the tenth and in my mind final time. I could not suffer the loss and the pain any longer. For some reason things felt different this time around even though I had bleeding, the symptoms that you expect to mean miscarriage. I was convinced this time that the bleeding didn't matter. The day after my bleeding I was scanned and to my astonishment I was carrying non-identical twin girls.

I went on to thirty-one weeks, when I went into spontaneous labour and delivered my babies naturally myself, with no pain relief, in four hours. During this time I felt calm and in control and had Ella (3lb 4oz) and Abigail (3lb 10oz) both breathing in air within twenty-four hours. There were no bright lights or signs but I felt strongly my angel was watching over me and my twins.

When the twins were twenty weeks old they were at home one night sleeping in their double buggy. At the time it was the only place they would sleep and we needed them to sleep! For no particular reason

127

instinct told me to check on them at around one a.m. They were not crying but I felt I had to check. When I went to them I found Abigail on the nursery floor five feet away from her buggy and completely happy, lying on her belly. Her covers were neatly folded across the buggy where Ella was sleeping soundly.

My grandmother had recently died and Abigail was the only twin she got to hold. I believe there was a reason Abigail was moved to the floor that night. Perhaps she was in danger of being smothered or perhaps she did fall and an angel caught her. It was definitely the work of an angel because to fall out of a buggy and be five feet away when you can't crawl or roll is impossible. For me nothing that happened that night was a coincidence or an accident. It was proof once again that the universe can be a wonderful and beautiful place if we open our hearts and minds to it.

As Rebecca says so beautifully in her story, angels are constantly speaking to us through coincidences, intuition and unexplained events. Sometimes these coincidences are dramatic and life-saving and hard to ignore, as was the case for Pamela and perhaps Rebecca, but more often than not they are subtle and everyday, and if we aren't looking out for them they are easy to miss.

Everyday angels

Perhaps you find a feather on your path, perhaps you think of a rainbow and then you see one, perhaps a butterfly lands on your arm. Or perhaps you find a coin or see repetitive number sequences, or hear an angel song on the radio or see an angel cloud or the word angel in a magazine or as a pub sign. All these are sure-fire signs, especially during those times when your faith is being tested, or when you are grieving the loss of a loved one, that your angels are never far away. These small gifts are not just coincidence but a form of communication from your guardian angel that should be noticed and honoured.

Several months ago I was feeling very distressed because an old friend had passed away suddenly. I walked into my office and there was a stunning white feather – a good three inches long – lying on the floor. It hadn't been there five minutes before. It was a great comfort to me to know that the angels were supporting me at that difficult time.

Sasha wasn't looking for an angel sign to guide her but when it came she knew exactly what it meant. Here's her story:

Angel on my pillow

I have always believed in angels, even more so after my twin sister died in November 2005. About a month before my sister died – it was a car accident that took her from me – I had decided to move in with my boyfriend. I don't think my parents liked him very much; my sister certainly didn't like him very much and I wasn't sure what to do. I wanted to break out on my own but I didn't want to hurt everyone I loved in the process.

The night after I heard the ghastly news about my sister I was sobbing into my pillows in my room when I saw this absolutely perfect white feather. I picked it up and it seemed to glisten like white diamonds. It was so beautiful. I just knew in that instant that my sister

129

had put it there. Gently I placed it on my dressing table and looked under my bed for a special storage box. I didn't want to lose this feather but when I turned around the feather had vanished. I turned my room upside down looking for it but I couldn't find it anywhere. Where did it go?

Later that evening Dad came into my room with a cup of warm milk and some biscuits. He looked exhausted and was trying to stay strong for me. He sat down and held my hand and even though I thought I didn't have any tears left they kept on coming. He reached into his pocket to get me a tissue and as he did I noticed on his shoulder my perfect white feather. I tried to gently take it off him but it refused to budge. It was like it was stuck there. And then I knew what was going on. My sister didn't want me to leave home and move in with my boyfriend.

Turns out it was the right decision. When I told my boyfriend I needed to be there for Mum and Dad, and that at seventeen I was too young to think about settling down, he pretended he was okay with it; but a month later he dumped me and got engaged to someone else. He can't have loved me as much as I thought he did.

Even now, sometimes when I don't even ask for it, whenever I am going through times of trouble, outside our house or in my car I find a white feather and I'm not even looking. I truly believe these are signs that my angel sister is loving and guiding me, just like she did when she was alive.

It's often during times of loss that angel signs or 'calling cards' offer the deepest comfort, as Robin's story illustrates:

Glowing in the dark

When my grandmother was diagnosed with terminal cancer and given no more than a few months to live, I simply couldn't accept what I was being told. My nan had virtually raised me and my four brothers and I thought she was indestructible. Then about two months after her diagnosis she was rushed into hospital and died two hours later, before I had time to get to her. The hospital had called but I was working three hours away. It was horrible not even being able to say goodbye. I loved my nan very much.

I went home feeling distraught. All I could think about was my nan. Some of my friends came round and took me out for a drink. I didn't feel like it but they made me. While I was sitting there in the pub this white feather just came floating down from the ceiling. It landed in my beer glass. It made me chuckle because nan had always hated me drinking. I just knew it was her getting in touch with me in a way that only I would understand.

Anne Marie also believes her guardian angel sent her a sign from above:

Angel dust

I was in a relationship for seven years when my partner and I thought it was time we started trying for a baby. I got pregnant and was so happy until at just three months my partner woke up one morning and said he couldn't do this any more because there was so much he wanted to do with his life before settling down. So he left me alone and pregnant.

I cried a lot in my pregnancy. I had wanted this perfect family and now I was by myself. When I was seven months gone I went to my mum's house for her fiftieth birthday party. This was tough for me because I still felt very tearful. I didn't want Mum to see I had been crying so I put on a lot of make-up.

When I walked into Mum's house and saw everyone I felt this rush of warmth, love and comfort. I couldn't explain why. I sat down on the couch and was handed a beautiful card. As I opened the card gorgeous glitter poured all over my stomach. It was so soft and gentle. My mum told me it was angel dust and I believe her, because after mum's birthday my life turned around. I had cried from three to seven months in my pregnancy but from then on the only tears I cried were on the day my gorgeous daughter was born and the same loving warm feeling came over me again.

Maureen is in no doubt of the significance of the white feather she saw:

Lifeline

My husband Eric and I were married for forty-four years when he was diagnosed with prostate cancer. I can't tell you what a shock it was and how upsetting. Well, my story begins when Eric and I were watching a TV show about how white feathers can appear when someone dies. Not long after, in November 2003, my Eric passed away. I was devastated.

The following April my family said we should all go away to Tenerife, as that was the place that Eric and I loved going to every April. I'm sure it was what he wanted me to do. Of course I knew it was going to be upsetting and hard without him – and it was, until a strange thing happened.

I was on the patio of our apartment when a small but pure white feather landed on my hand. There wasn't a single bird in sight. I believe that was a sign of Eric's approval. I still have the feather and will never part with it. It's like my lifeline.

Naelene shared this interesting story with me:

Connections

When I married again it was to a lovely man called Roy. We had twelve years together before he passed on. He was in hospital for a while before he died. He was very ill and my daughter took me home to stay overnight with her. One night I lay in bed worrying. Beside the bed there was an antique telephone that was used only as an ornament. During his working years Roy was employed by a telephone company so he had a strong connection with phones. At quarter to five in the morning that unconnected phone rang twice. I could not believe it. I couldn't go back to sleep so I got up and sat on a window seat until my family all got up and I could tell them what had happened. Twelve hours later, at a quarter to five that afternoon, Roy passed away.

Naelene believes that the ringing of the unconnected phone that night was a sign from her guardian angel that her husband was soon to pass away, but even though he was going to another place the strong connection between them would never die.

For Kay the sign she was hoping for really did have wings:

133

Fly away

My dear father passed away fifteen years ago after suffering from cancer. He always loved birds and kept pigeons as a child. I can remember a time when he found a blackbird with a broken wing and nursed it back to health.

For many years my husband, who is of Arab origin, wanted me and my children to emigrate to Jordan with him. My father was always worried about us leaving. When the time finally came close for us to leave I remember one day thinking a lot about the move when out of the blue a robin appeared in front of me. Another time, I was terribly worried about a major operation I was scheduled to have; then my daughter told me there was a robin sitting on the window singing – in the middle of June in Jordan! I'm sure this was a message from my dad trying to comfort me. Another time it was New Year's Eve and my mother was at the kitchen window when again a robin sat on the window singing.

I would also like to share another story, about my daughter's wedding day. A few days before the big day I was in the car with my sister with the windows closed when there was an overwhelming scent of fresh flowers. We both said together, 'Can you smell flowers?' We think it was Dad saying, 'Give Layla some flowers from me.'

Although I receive the most letters and emails about white feathers – and they are indeed one of the commonly reported angel signs, of course – angels don't just restrict themselves to white feathers or indeed other common angel signs, such as phones ringing mysteriously, repetitive number sequences, the discovery of lost objects or coins, sightings of birds, stunning rainbows or angel-shaped clouds, the sudden overwhelming scent of flowers or overheard meaningful songs or the word or name angel when we least expect it.

All these are commonly reported signs that appear at significant or meaningful times in our lives to remind us that we are not alone, but I believe it's possible to see reassuring angel signs all around you, if you just open your eyes and look, and in Chapter Seven we'll explore in more detail this theme of everyday angel signs and how to ask for, notice and bring their healing power into your life.

Touched by light

Not only do I believe in angels but also I believe in the everyday miracles of healing, love and comfort they bring into our lives through coincidences, intuition, signs and answered prayers. We may not always be able to see angels, because they exist in a realm we humans cannot even begin to comprehend, but I hope the stories in this chapter will have inspired you to believe that in some form or other they are always out there listening, under-standing, answering our prayers and touching our hearts with their light. I'm not talking about in-your-face apparitions and visions, but rather those small miracles of positive outcomes and the discovery of hope, courage and love when all seems lost. Appreciate these things for what they are: not everything can be explained away by coincidence or chance. And above all trust that still voice within, the voice of your intuition – or, as I like to think of it, your guardian angel whispering to you.

CHAPTER 5

Divine Collisions

> The golden moments in the stream of life
> rush past us and we see nothing but sand; the
> angels come to visit us, and we only know
> them when they are gone
>
> George Eliot

Be prepared for the stories in this chapter to sink deep into your heart and mind. They aren't about a mysterious voice, blinding lights, vivid dreams or white feathers floating down. As incredible as these things are, when the life of a loved one or your own life is saved by an angel the wonder of it can be overwhelming. The true stories in this chapter go way beyond coincidence. In each case 'something' truly extraordinary occurred that healed or saved a life. This 'something' might have been a strong warning or a mysterious stranger who appeared out of nowhere at just the right time. In other instances even more unusual things happened.

For many people the explanation of angelic or divine intervention is all that is needed. Others find answers by arguing the scientific reality that everything in this life and the next is connected and that time is an illusion. There is no past, present or future, no reality or non-reality, just our perception. No matter the explanation for the kind of miracles you are about to read it's impossible not to be inspired and energized by the magic and wonder of it all.

Let's begin with a couple of medical miracles that hit the head-lines in the past few years:

Polish worker wakes to a world of democracy, mobile phones and abundant choice

A Polish railway worker who fell into a coma in 1988 – a year before the fall of communism – woke up nineteen years later in April 2007 to a world of democracy, mobile phones and abundant choice and said that he is amazed to find that people still complain. Jan Grzebski, sixty-five, was cared for at home by his wife, Gertruda. She turned him over several times a day to prevent him getting bed sores. He had lost consciousness after being hit by a train. He is in no doubt of his debt to his wife. 'It was Gertruda who saved me, and I'll never forget it,' he said. 'I cried a lot, and I prayed a lot,' Mrs Grzebski said.

As we've seen in this book there are many kinds of miracle heal-ing. Some occur when even the most optimistic of persons loses all hope. There are also cases when people who have been declared clinically dead are restored to life. Sometimes this happens in hosp-tial but there are even cases when it has occurred in mortuaries. Lazarus syndrome cases, which have been noted dozens of times in medical literature, are shocking and compelling because they force us to open our minds and question once again what we believe to be possible and what we believe to be impossible.

Coma-recovery stories and cases of people who have been declared dead come back to life are popular with the media. These are such rare occurrences and whenever they happen there is always talk of miracles and divine intervention, because all too often they prove that medical assessment regarding the level of awareness experienced by the coma victim or the person declared dead might have been wrong.

This is what defines a miracle. As already discussed, by definition a miracle is something that appears to be inexplicable by the laws of nature as we have come to understand them. A miracle is therefore both awe-inspiring and humbling because it reminds us that, even though we may believe our knowledge to be advancing, our understanding of the laws of nature, and indeed life and death, remains limited and we have been putting restrictions on the miraculous power of love.

This next story, sent in by John, provides yet another demonstration of the healing and miraculous power of love:

Split second

When I was growing up I was very close to my paternal grandfather. He used to take me fishing. I've never known such peace as I had in the happy hours I spent with him. Sometimes we would chat. Other times we would just sit together. I liked being with him. He made me feel good. I loved him.

I lost him, though, when I was twelve. He didn't die or anything but my mum and dad split up and I went to live with Mum and she didn't want me to see my grandfather any more. I know he tried, because I used to hear the phone ringing and the doorbell ringing. I knew it was him. He probably missed me as much as I missed him but trying to get through my mum was like trying to get through a brick wall. The next time I saw him I was about fourteen. He didn't look very well and told me he was going to go and live in the country to get his health back. I asked for his address and he said he would give it to me but he never did. Perhaps he did and my mum didn't give it to me. I guess I'll never know as my mum died three years ago and after the divorce I never heard from my dad again.

I didn't seen my grandfather again until I was twenty-five. I was coming home from work and the tube station was really busy. The platform was crowded and everyone was jostling forward. There was a train approaching and I was at the front of the queue so I tried to step backwards but everyone was pushing against me. For a split second I thought I was going to die because I started to fall forward. I didn't fall, though, because I felt these strong arms behind me pulling me back. I turned around and there was my grandfather. He looked really healthy and happy. I couldn't believe it. I was just about to talk to him but then a sea of people crowded between us and I was pushed into the carriage. I tried to look out for him but couldn't see him anywhere.

When I got home I was desperate to contact him. I guess I was lonely and he was the only happy memory from my childhood. I did a lot of internet searching and made a lot of phone calls and was even-tually able to track him down. Turns out he lived only a few minutes' drive away from me in a residential care home. As soon as I found out I jumped into my car and drove to visit him.

When I arrived and asked for him I got the shock of my life. Apparently my grandfather had died the very evening that I had seen him at the tube station. Nobody believes me when I tell them this story but I know it to be true. Some people say the man on the platform must have been someone who looked like my grandfather but I'm in no doubt it was him.

Nancy shared a kind of similar story with me:

Gliding

I lost my mother when I was five and I believe she came back to save me from drowning in the summer of 1995. I was having fun on the beach with my sister. It was a glorious day and I didn't hesitate jumping into the sea. I soon realized what a mistake I had made. The current was strong and I was drowning. My sister is a stronger swimmer than me and I could hear her screaming for me. It was the most terrifying moment of my life. I was going to die. I just knew it.

I didn't die, though, because just as I was out of breath I felt a sense of peace come over me. It's hard to explain. I also saw my mother in the water beneath me. She placed her arms around my legs and pushed me up. Just before I surfaced she smiled at me and then I found myself floating on the surface of the water towards the beach. It was as if I was resting on a giant float because I wasn't moving my arms and legs. I was gliding to safety.

I thought I was hallucinating or something but when my sister came running to me and I saw the look on her face I knew something incredible had happened. She told me that one moment I had disappeared under the water and the next I had appeared on the beach. It was impossible. We both started to cry because we knew that a miracle had saved me.

I have received a number of letters from people who tell me that they have been carried or lifted to safety. Like Nancy, Honey, whose story is below, has no idea how it happened:

Falling down

The first day I moved into my new home I was busy unpacking until late in the evening. I stood on the kitchen units – which were quite high – to put up the curtains. I stepped backwards and fell back on the stone floor. However, I seemed to fall in slow motion. I'm quite a big girl and when I fall I fall with a thud, but I landed gently on my back without a scratch on me. I often wonder if someone caught me and gently lowered me. I'll never know but my heart tells me I was supported.

Sherry believes she witnessed something extraordinary when her daughter tripped and fell:

Strong presence

When my daughter was twenty months old I took her along to a parents' meeting at my eight-year-old son's junior school. We had to climb a large flight of stairs and she insisted on having a go so it took ages, as she hadn't been walking that long. We took breaks between levels.

I must have turned my back for just a second because when I looked around I saw her running back down the stairs. Before I could get to her she tripped and started to fall but before her head hit the step something caught her and slowly pushed her back into an upright position so she could get her balance back. When I got to her she was standing completely still. I couldn't see anything but I felt a strong presence and I truly believe her guardian angel stopped her falling and hitting her head.

As strange as it may seem sometimes accidents can bring about miracles.

You've probably read or heard about heart-stopping stories of people who have survived against all odds after falling from great heights when their parachute failed to open. Words such as mind-boggling or miraculous are often used to describe these incidents. For many people divine intervention appears to be the only explanation for such incredible stories and it is certainly the only answer that Susan could find when she found herself moments from death. Here's her story:

Angel wings

I'm going back to 1981 now. I was driving my car. It was dark and all of a sudden my headlights went out. I could hear a lot of noise and sparking from the engine. I did notice signs on the street saying no stopping or parking so my first instinct was to get out of the car as fast as I could. Then just as I was getting out of the driver's seat I knew it was all over because a large white bus hit my car. I closed my eyes and heard a swishing sound but when I opened them again and looked up I was fine. I could not believe it. For a moment I thought I was dead and I was simply watching the scene unfold. But I wasn't dead. The bus had pulled up alongside my car and the driver was shouting at me. I think he was shaken up too by what happened because he thought he had killed me. I couldn't say anything to him; I was just in shock.

The noise I heard sounded like angel wings covering me as the bus ran into me. As long as I live I will never forget that night. I was pregnant at the time with my son and it terrifies me to think that I might not only have lost my life but lost him as well.

This next story was reported in the local press at the time. I've paraphrased it here because it's yet another powerful testimony to the healing power of angels. As you'll read, the boy involved has an unshakeable belief that an angel saved his life:

Teen says an angel saved him

On Friday 23 November 2007, nineteen-year-old Joshua Kosch was hit by a freight train in downtown Fayetteville and doctors amputated his right leg. Kosch said he saw an angel who helped him survive the accident.

The boy had got dressed up in Victorian attire and was walking to A Dickens Holiday, an annual downtown festival. He stood on one set of railroad tracks near Hay Street while waiting for a southbound train to pass him on the adjoining tracks. According to his parents he did not hear the northbound train approaching him. Although the train had slowed to about twenty mph, and despite his best efforts, the conductor could not stop the ninety-three-car train in time to avoid hitting Kosch. Kosch said he remembered seeing an angel during the accident. 'He [the angel] told me it wasn't my time,' Kosch said. 'And I couldn't get up. And that's because he held me down.'

Kosch spent several weeks in intensive care at Cape Fear Valley Medical Center, recovering from rib fractures, broken vertebrae, a broken arm and a punctured lung. His right leg was amputated above his knee. His mother, Barbara, said seeing her son survive has been a miracle.

Pamela sent me this story about her brother. It wasn't reported in the press but, like all the unreported stories in this book, it is nonetheless incredible:

Trapped

My brother once had a very lucky escape from a car crash when he was a young teenager. My mother firmly believes it was his angel who saved him. The car flipped over on a notorious road in Scotland and my brother was unconscious and trapped upside down in the car.

When he woke up he couldn't get the seatbelt off to help himself or his friend. He was terrified because he could smell petrol around him and he was trapped. He closed his eyes and hoped that someone would help and all of a sudden he felt calmness. He simply moved himself to the side a little and the seatbelt came undone, enabling him to get himself and his friend to a place of safety.

Jamail has this story to tell:

This is it

It was late and my wife had just called to tell me to hurry home from work so although I was certainly not speeding I was probably driving much faster than I should have been. I can recall every second of the accident. Suddenly, this car pulled in front of me and I was forced to slam on my brakes to avoid crashing into him. I thought this was it. I was going to die and I was going to die horribly.

I jerked my steering wheel hard to try to minimize the damage and I managed to avoid a head-on collision, but in the process my car started to spin across the road and I hit a wall there. The accident couldn't have been much worse and everyone on the scene said it was a miracle I was alive or not seriously injured.

I didn't tell anyone when I gave my statements because I was already in trouble for driving too fast and I didn't want to make things worse by talking about divine intervention, but I want to tell you what I really experienced in those seconds my car went out of control. I felt this hand covering my face, protecting it and holding me in my seat so I didn't fly out. I simply felt that someone was helping me and that this wasn't it. It wasn't my time.

Elaine also believes it wasn't her time. She emailed me this stunning account:

Move over

I was driving down the motorway and although it wasn't late it was dark because we were in the run-up to Christmas and the shorter days.

There was a lot of traffic in every lane so everyone was forced to travel at around the same speed.

I didn't try to overtake as a lot of people seemed to be trying to do because I couldn't see the point. As I was getting ready to take a turn to the left off the motorway, all of a sudden I saw the bright lights of a truck flashing ahead of me. It must have stalled. I looked in my mirrors to see if I could overtake it but the cars behind me were coming so fast I couldn't do anything without bashing into the truck. My car is only a Volkswagen and the truck was huge. It would have eaten me up but if I changed lane I would cause a multi-car accident.

It all happened so fast. I remember being paralysed with fear and just shutting my eyes and praying I would be saved. The next moment, I couldn't believe it: I had moved over into the other lane. I thought I would be involved in a crash but there I was driving. The car hadn't been in my control. Something or someone else did the moving over for me.

Sometimes collisions with the divine aren't invisible to the human eye, as was the case for Pamela, Joshua and Elaine. Sometimes our guardian angels do allow themselves to be seen by us in a very real way, which brings us nicely to stories about mysterious strangers.

Mysterious strangers

In the last few chapters some of the stories have already touched on yet another way in which angels can communicate their message of love and healing to us, and which I've often encountered in my research: the phenomenon of mysterious strangers who seem to appear out of nowhere to offer healing and assistance during times of illness or crisis. When attempts are made to locate the person who has been the helper, there is no one present who fits the description. The stranger seems to have vanished.

I'm often asked whether these people are angels. It's impossible to be certain but when I've spoken to the people involved and discussed the details of what occurred this often seems to be the only plausible explanation. As I've received so many stories of this kind, I'm convinced that angels do appear in this way and when this happens the human and divine worlds collide. I believe angels choose this form so that people in danger or crisis feel reassured by the familiarity of a fellow human being and don't have any idea that this is an angelic encounter until after the event.

Even though these mysterious strangers tend to appear and disappear out of nowhere at pivotal moments to offer comfort and physical assistance, there is always the argument that they are simply good Samaritans reluctant to appear in the spotlight. But whoever and whatever they are you'll have a hard time convincing the people who sent me their true stories that they are not angels. People like Vivian, who gives her account below:

Angels on the main road

Six years ago, when I was twenty-two, I was involved in a seven-car pile-up on a main road. I found out later that it was caused by an exhausted lorry driver who ran a red light.

I shall never forget the smell of petrol and blood that night. I didn't feel any pain. I've been told you don't. Your body goes into shock and painkilling chemicals flood your system. When I put the brakes on I had been frantically trying to change gear with my left hand, and I did see that three of the fingers on my left hand were now hanging by a thread.

My first thought was for my four-year-old son, Shaun. I prayed that he would be spared. I struggled to turn around but there was mangled metal everywhere. Eventually I managed to turn my head. I saw the seat where he had been sitting caved in. There was broken glass everywhere. He wasn't there. My heart stopped. He must have been thrown out of the front window. I tried to scream out to him but no words came out of my mouth. All I could do was sit there in blood, metal and helpless agony until the firemen arrived to cut me out.

I kept telling the firemen to forget about me and find Shaun. They searched in the back and didn't find him. There had been no damage to the seat belt so I think they thought I had gone crazy and hadn't had any passengers in the back. I was asked if I had been drinking and when I said I'd had a glass for lunch of course they got suspicious. There was so much to do on the scene they took me to the ambulance waiting area and moved on quickly.

I wasn't going to wait anywhere; I was going to find my son. So as soon as they lost sight of me I started to run around desperately asking anybody who would listen if they had seen Shaun. He had been wearing his Thomas the Tank Engine top and jeans and white trainers.

After the longest few minutes of my life, I found Shaun sitting quietly by himself. He had a nasty gash on his forehead, which someone had hastily bandaged to stop the blood flow, but other than that he was fine. When I asked him how he got there and who had helped him Shaun told me that his daddy had put him there and taken care of his head. Then he'd told him to wait patiently until his mum would come and take them home.

At the time I knew this was impossible because Shaun's dad had died just over a year previously. I thought he must have been mistaken but later, when we were at the hospital, I tried to thank the paramedic who had taken care of Shaun but nobody came forward. When I questioned the police and the firemen on the scene and told them that I really did have a child travelling with me that night, none of them owned up to helping Shaun. None of them could also explain how Shaun had survived the car crash and got out of the car in one piece.

Perhaps it was just a passing stranger but I don't think that's possible because there are no pavements on the road I was travelling on and it was miles away from any shops or walking areas. My only source of reference is Shaun, who later told me that when his daddy kissed his forehead he stopped feeling any pain. He also told me that he had begged his daddy not to go but his daddy had said that he had to go but would always be watching over him.

Shaun's ten now and everyone tells me he is the spitting image of his father. The likeness takes my breath away. He tells me he can't remember anything about that night. It makes me sad that memories of his dad have faded away now but I'm happy to know that somewhere deep down inside him he knows that an angel saved his life and kissed away his pain.

Carolyn in the US also believes there was an angel on the road:

Who was she?

It was the evening of Sunday 21 January 2001 at around six forty. I was on the way from Winn-Dixie, where I was working, heading home. I was turning left at a yellow light, confidently thinking that the truck twenty-five to thirty feet away was going to come to a stop. WRONG! The truck hit the passenger side of my little 1989 Hyundai at forty to fifty mph. I remember the truck hitting my vehicle in slow motion.

I was awakened by the touch of a presence upon my face, by a lady with red hair. Being that she was on the passenger side (which was struck by the truck) looking into the vehicle, I knew that she didn't reach in and touch me, but it was like a spiritual connection. She said, 'You've just been in an accident. Everything is okay. The ambulance is on the way.' I never noticed her leave the side of my car. It was like a minute or less after our conversation that the police and ambulance were pulling up. There was only one witness. He claimed he saw everything, having been behind me. I told everyone about the lady with red hair, and they said there was only one witness to the accident, which was the man. My mom says it was my guardian angel.

Judy truly believes healing angels have been at work in her life. Here's a section of the email she sent over to me:

Don't move

This happened to me several winters ago. The experience has left me with scars that will last a lifetime but I've also been left in no doubt that angels exist.

It was about seven o'clock in the evening and I had just finished cashing up in my shop – I sell flowers. It had been quite a busy day and takings had been good. I heard this knock on the door. I ignored it at first because I was in a hurry to get home – it was my son's birthday party at the weekend and I had a lot to do. The knocking was persistent so eventually I went to see who it was. I saw a man standing outside and he looked fairly frantic. I told him I was closed now but he begged me to open up just for a few minutes so he could buy his fiancée some flowers. He told me it was the anniversary of their first meeting today and if he didn't come home with some flowers he would be toast.

I refused at first but then I felt sorry for him and let him in. It was a stupid thing to do. Within seconds of me opening the door two other guys appeared alongside him and pushed me to the ground. I didn't stand a chance. As one of them raided my till, the other two hit and kicked me until I was almost unconscious. I wasn't putting up a fight and I remember telling them to just take the money, so I don't know why they had to be so brutal.

When they left me I was virtually unconscious. I had several cracked ribs, bruising everywhere and my skull was fractured from the kicking they gave me. Dimly aware that I needed to get to a hospital fast I tried to inch myself towards my bag to get my mobile phone. It was impossible to see because of the blood in my eyes. I began to use my elbows to push me forward but then I felt a gentle pressure on my arms and I heard the voice of a woman telling me to stay still and not to move. I was overcome with relief that someone had found me and rested my broken head on the floor. Then the voice told me that help would be on its way soon. Then everything went black.

When I woke up I was in hospital. My doctor told me that things could have been a lot worse if I had tried to move about after my beating. Because I had kept my fractured skull relatively still my vision, though it would never be perfect, wouldn't be lost completely. I told him that I needed to thank the paramedic lady who found me for that. The doctor looked puzzled and told me that my husband had found me alone that evening and called the emergency services and two male paramedics were dispatched. He had decided to surprise me with a lift home (normally I walk). When I spoke to my husband he told me that I was already unconscious when he found me.

Sometimes I wonder if I imagined it all, but other times I remember how I had tried to struggle to get to my mobile and how this quiet, calming and reassuring voice had kept me still. I will never forget it for as long as I live. It gives me hope that as horrible as my experience with those thugs was, something or someone was watching over me.

This next angel was clearly seen by a group of friends but afterwards just seemed to vanish. Once again we as readers are challenged to ask if it was a real angel or a human angel. Sometimes it can be hard to know the answer but Doreen, who sent me this story, knows what she believes:

Submerged

I was at my local swimming pool with a bunch of my friends. We were larking about as usual and having a great time. I can't remember all the details but we were playing silly games and trying to grab each other from under the water. I was just about to dive down when someone grabbed my legs and pulled me under. Then in an instant a whole crowd of my friends seemed to create a wall on top of me. There were arms and legs everywhere. I couldn't get past them and I started to panic and take in water. I must have blacked out but I saw this woman lifeguard swim down to me and then she dragged me to the surface. Then I was on the side of the pool and she was making me spit out water. My friends were all freaking out because I wasn't breathing but eventually, with this lady's help, I came back.

When I came back my friends mobbed me again. They were just so relieved that I hadn't died, but a male lifeguard pushed them away from me and helped me to my feet. He had a mobile in his hand and phoned for an ambulance. I told him I didn't need one, that I was okay, but he insisted. I turned around to thank the lady who had rescued me but she was nowhere to be seen. I asked the male lifeguard where she was and he said that there were no female lifeguards. I asked my friends and they told me that they hadn't seen her leave. We looked around the pool, which had been quickly evacuated because of my emergency, but there was no one there.

What's strange is that none of us could remember what this woman looked like even though all of us had seen her pulling me out of the water and saving my life. Nobody could describe what she was wearing, what the colour of her hair was or anything. It felt like she had not existed or that we had all seen her without really looking.

It's certainly possible that everyone was so wrapped up in the drama of the moment that no one involved remembered what this lady looked like. But, as Doreen points out, it does seem very strange that no one would remember the face of a lady who dragged a young girl out of the water, knelt down beside her and brought her back to life. Normally during times of extreme crisis our memories of the events are heightened, not dimmed.

Talking of memories, Tina will never forget the eyes of a stranger who carried her to safety:

Everything to plan

I was eight months pregnant and on my way home from work. It was raining very, very hard and I must have slipped and fallen. There I was splashing around in a huge puddle with blood on my knees when this man came up to me. He looked like a homeless man and he had the greenest and clearest eyes I have ever seen. He asked me what I was doing out in this weather. He could tell I was pregnant because of the bulge under my coat. I could barely see him because I had my hood on against all the rain. I couldn't walk so he picked me up. I must have weighed a ton as I'm a well-built girl and had put on a good thirty pounds with my pregnancy.

This man carried me all the way to my train station and got me there just as the train was moments from leaving. Then he helped me inside and told me to visit my doctor as soon as I got home to make sure I hadn't hurt my baby in the fall. I looked down for a second to undo my coat and take my hood off so I could thank this man properly but when I looked up there was no one there. What was even stranger was that there was no puddle of water where he had been standing like there was under my boots. He was just gone, like a puff of smoke.

I knew he had to be my angel protecting my unborn son. What other explanation could there be? I went to the doctor immediately and the next morning my baby was induced. Apparently his head was getting a bit too large and my doctor said that as I was only a few weeks away from my due date it would be easier for me and safer for my son if he was delivered early. Again I think this was all in my angel's plan to ensure the safety and wellbeing of my unborn son and me.

But what about stories of people who don't appear out of nowhere or disappear into thin air but come in the normal way to perform a miracle of healing or give assistance at just the right time, and then leave in a perfectly ordinary manner? Stories like this one below, sent to me by Esther:

Tough love

If I hadn't sat by this guy I'd never met before I might not be writing to you now. I was out celebrating my birthday with my mum and my three sisters. I'd ordered some curry and it tasted delicious. I must have crammed a lot into my mouth because I felt myself swallow really hard. Then I coughed and tried to breathe and realized that something had got stuck in my windpipe. All of a sudden I couldn't speak or breathe. It was like a nightmare. I could just about cough but this wasn't helping. I started to lose consciousness and then I felt these really tough slaps on my back. They really hurt. I was too weak to struggle back. I just collapsed forward. The slaps continued and then I felt the meat in my throat move and I could breathe again.

I owe my life to the man who sat with his wife and young son on the table next to me. I'm deeply grateful to him. He is so modest about what he has done. He told me that at first he thought I was messing about, because we were quite a noisy table, but then he knew something was seriously wrong. Mercifully, he had completed a first-aid course the month previously and knew exactly what to do. Mum and my sisters would not have known how to help me.

The experience has encouraged me to learn some life-saving skills of my own. I'd like to think that I could help if someone was in a similar situation. I think there can be no better feeling than knowing you have saved a person's life.

It's incredibly heart-warming to read stories about people stepping forward to help or heal other people in times of need or crisis. So much of what we read in the newspapers these days is depressing or distressing, but every so often if you look out for them you can find inspiring stories about passers-by with remarkable selflessness, courage and healing powers. Stories like these – all reported in the summer and autumn of 2009, as I write this book – that can fill us with a much-needed sense of hope and pride in human nature because they remind us that angels can and do appear in human form.

Good samaritans save pensioner's life

A Scottish pensioner whose husband suffered a heart attack while enjoying a day out with their grandson has thanked passers-by who battled to save his life. Ann Tait, sixty-nine, and husband Archie, seventy-two, had been spending time with their three-year-old grandson, Matthew, at a play park when Archie collapsed and fell on to the road. Luckily there was a young couple in their twenties passing and the woman worked at the Royal Infirmary. She and her husband gave Archie CPR. An ambulance happened to be driving past at the time and it stopped, and the paramedics helped the couple. Everything just fell into place. The father of three has now left the hospital and is recovering at home.

Mysterious strangers save a young boy's life

A mother whose twelve-year-old son was knocked down by a car has sent a heartfelt message of thanks to the people who saved his life. Jack Billington was out with friends when he was struck by a vehicle. Three mystery passers-by came to his aid. His mother said: 'They always say that the first hour after a road accident can mean the difference between life and death. I owe the people who came to the aid of my son a huge debt — he's incredibly lucky to be alive.' Jack was then airlifted to hospital where doctors discovered he had a fractured pelvis.

Passer-by saves newborn baby and toddler from a burning building today as their parents screamed for help

Stephen Blackman, fifty, from Waltham Abbey, Essex, was pasting up a poster near Edmonton Green railway station when he saw flames coming from an off-licence in Church Street and heard a man shouting. Mr Blackman ran towards the blaze with his ladder. He saw a woman at the window of the flat above the shop. She had a bundle in her arms. It was a baby. He climbed up, tucked the baby under his arm and also carried down a three-year-old boy. The children's parents climbed down the ladder after him seconds before fire engines arrived. The family tried to thank him but he just shrugged his shoulders as if to say 'no problem' and walked off. Ten people were treated for smoke inhalation and it took twenty firemen two hours to tackle the blaze, the cause of which is under investigation.

Passer-by saves a child's life

A passer-by saved the life of a six-year-old boy when he caught the child after he accidentally fell from a seventh-floor apartment in Gothenburg, Sweden. Two police officers on patrol near the building were unable to save the boy as they approached the building, but his fall was broken by an unnamed member of the public. According to police spokesperson Pia Goksöyr: 'The boy had already fallen. There was a man who saw the boy hanging from the window and tried to catch him. The man succeeded in partially catching him. It may be that the boy shut himself in his room to be by himself and the parents outside the door in the apartment were unaware of what had happened.' The boy was taken to Sahlgrenska University Hospital before being moved to Sahlgrenska's Queen Silvia Children's Hospital, where his condition has been described as serious but stable.

Even though the mysterious strangers in these stories certainly behaved like angels they were most likely ordinary human beings acting with courage and selflessness. All that could be said here is that sometimes angels can use ordinary people as conscious or unconscious vehicles for their healing. At the end of the day does it really matter if angels speak to us in human or divine form?

The best policy, in my opinion, is always to treat strangers as if they were angels because what I have heard, read and seen over the years makes me truly believe that angels walk among us in human form. Just think how exciting life could become if you are always wondering whether the people you have met or are about to meet are angels in disguise.

Whether human or divine, stories about mysterious strangers or passers-by who save lives remind me of a time when the world was a safer place because of a stronger community spirit. It wasn't considered mad or bad to talk to or befriend people we didn't know or lend assistance in times of need. People are susceptible to the scaremongering around stranger danger because we live in a society that has lost faith in itself and in which people are losing faith and trust in each other. Of course, we need to be sensible and use our common sense, and not invade the personal space of others or put our lives at risk, but we also want to be happy, healthy and well adjusted and to do this we need to learn to trust each other just a little bit more.

Reading or hearing stories about mysterious strangers or passers-by – or, as I often like to call them, 'angels in disguise' – can help restore some of that faith and trust we used to have in each other. I sincerely hope it will encourage you to reach out and connect with those around you with love and trust. It doesn't have to be much: a friendly smile, an offer to help or a moment or two to chat is often enough. As Pam's story illustrates so well, these simple gestures can make a world of difference to those who receive them:

Tough day

It was a tough day for me. I was trying to stay away from the drink and coping with the loss of my job and my baby; I'd miscarried the previous month. My family was trying to help me and I was seeing a counsellor but what made the difference was a stranger on a bike. He must have seen me parked on the road. I was crying with my head on the steering wheel. He cycled up to me and tapped on my window and asked me if I was okay. I said I was but he looked at me and asked me if I was sure. I nodded and forced a smile and then he said, 'Okay, take care now.'

That simple interaction instantly lifted my spirits. I told him to take care of himself too, as the roads were busy. As he cycled off he looked round once more to check on me and I smiled and waved to him.

As I started up the engine I wondered if he was an angel sent to check up on me. This person who I didn't know and have never seen again made me feel so cared for and at ease with life. Him just stopping like that – taking time out of his day for me – was all I needed to know that my guardian angel had connected with me.

Every day of our lives there are windows of opportunity to make someone else's life easier or harder. I personally believe that easing another person's mind and heart not only feeds their spirit but also strengthens your own connection with the angels.

At this point I can think of no better place to include this short but perfect story. In my writing about angels I find myself returning to it time and time again and it never fails to inspire and educate me.

On the street I saw a little boy cold and shivering in a thin pair of shorts and a threadbare shirt. I got angry and asked my angels, 'Why did you permit this? Why don't you do something about it?'

My angel replied, 'I certainly did do something about it – I brought you here.'

This story is a powerful reminder that angels don't just exist in the courage and kindness of others – they can exist within each of us. If you don't feel angels working in your life one of the best ways to discover them is from the inside out. You may not realize it but everything you say and do can touch those around you in a divine way. Just feeling love or compassion for others is angelic. A kind word can help someone see the goodness around them; an act of kindness can bring beauty into another person's life and restore their faith in human nature and in themselves.

Although we may never save lives in a dramatic way we can still all aspire to be angels in disguise, bringing laughter and comfort to those who cross our paths. I always appreciate it when a stranger smiles at me for no reason other than to connect with me. There is nothing she wants in return except a friendly smile, which I happily give. If we could all reach out to help one another and then teach this to our children imagine the angelic effect that would have on everyone and everything. Imagine how much easier it would be for the angels to bring their unconditional love and goodness into the world.

And while we are on the subject of unconditional love I'd like to close this chapter by talking about another kind of angel in disguise that can intervene at just the right moment to save or heal a person's life. Animals may not be able to talk to us but the stories I have gathered leave me in no doubt that not only can they communicate in ways we don't expect but also that the love and devotion they offer us in this life and the next has the power to heal.

Animal angels

Even if an animal or pet does not rescue or heal their owner in a dramatic way, I know from my own experience with animals and from the stories I have read from animal lovers that owning a pet can have a positive impact on your life. My cats haven't thrown themselves in front of a raging dog to save me or pawed at my face to wake me up so I can escape a fire (although there are stories about cats performing such courageous acts), but they have brought a lot of love, laughter and companionship into my life. They have also comforted me when I have felt unwell or depressed and their devotion and love has melted my heart when I needed it the most.

I'm often asked if animals are angels. I can't answer that because I don't have all the answers but I can say with confidence that pets can teach us a great deal about the power of unconditional love. Just imagine what a lonely and bleak place the world would be without animals. The world would lose so much love; and love, remember, is where you can always find angels.

I enjoyed this story sent to me by Kirstie. I hope you enjoy it too:

Rupert

Rupert was our family dog. He was such a special dog. He came to us at a time when we were all at our lowest. We had lost Dad about two years beforehand. He had a massive heart attack and died aged only forty-four. I was only thirteen when my dad died and my brother was only ten. Two years after his death we had moved into a new house and we all really wanted a new dog; we got an Old English sheepdog and called him Rupert.

Rupert was so loving and caring. He made us laugh so much, which is what we all really needed. Mum and I felt like some part of Dad had returned to us to inject a bit of joy into our lives again. One of the funniest things was when we tried to teach him to bark at the back door when he needed to be let out but all he ended up doing was just sitting there and opening and closing his mouth. It was so funny and a goldfish comes to mind. No matter what mood you were in, you just couldn't help but laugh.

There's so much more that he did in addition to bringing laughter back into our house. When I was at college I lost my best friend to cystic fibrosis. She passed away in hospital and I was told the sad news by my tutors – we were on the same course at the time. I was in total shock. After losing my dad I didn't think I could feel as heartbroken as that again, but I did. After I found out I was completely lost and walked around as if I didn't know where I was, but when I got home

Rupert was waiting by the front door for me. He hadn't done that before. He was always in his bed or in his favourite corner. I could hardly get through the door with him trying to jump on me. It was as if he knew and I didn't have to explain anything to him. He clung to me like glue and cuddled up to me as if to give me a hug. He was even reluctant to go out on his walk, which he loved, if I wasn't going along. This went on till long after my friend's funeral and then slowly he went back to normal, but if I ever felt low again he would sense it and be at my side like a shot.

Kirstie's story is special because it shows how the devotion and care of an animal angel can be so comforting and healing. Angel's story is also special, because it shows that as long as there is love the connection between an animal and his or her owner is unbreakable:

Burning bright

Tiger was my baby. She was the most stunningly beautiful Persian cross you can imagine. She also had the loudest purr you could imagine – now I know why they call them purrsians. I lived with Tiger and loved her every second of the five years we spent together but she got very ill and needed to be put to sleep.

One morning I was sitting in my chair drinking my tea and watching breakfast TV when I felt something jump on the back of the sofa and brush past my neck. Then I felt something kneading my left shoulder. Tiger always used to do that when she was alive. It was part of our morning ritual. I also felt warmth, happiness and light all around me.

I wasn't daydreaming or dreaming. I didn't imagine it. Tiger came back for one last goodbye.

After my first cat, Crystal, died I would often sense her presence or feel the brush of her body against my legs. I was never frightened by these experiences – quite the contrary, they seemed the most comforting and natural thing in the world. And the more stories I hear from people who have had similar experiences the more convinced I am that contact with a beloved deceased pet is scannot break the bonds of love that can be created between human and animal.

Some people struggle with the idea that animals can survive death, arguing that animals don't have souls or spirits as humans do. But animals are made of the same energy that humans are made of and in my mind there is no reason why they may not survive in the same way. Anyone who has ever bonded with a pet will be aware of the strong, sometimes psychic connection that can exist. It's as if our pets sense our moods, read our minds and heal our hearts. Psychic energy could very possibly be part of the same energy as spiritual energy and so animals could have as much connection to the world of spirit as humans. Perhaps more so, given their often superior sense of taste, smell, sight and hearing and their ability to sense what is unseen.

Pets don't ask much from us. They simply ask for our love and gentleness and in return they love us unconditionally and watch over us in this life and the next. I don't know whether animals are angels but all this sounds a great deal like an angel to me.

I'd like to end this chapter with one more animal story. I'm including it here because the stories in the next chapter are all about death and the afterlife and this story, sent to me by Ron, shows that it is not always human death, or brief glimpses of the afterlife, that can change our perspective on life. Sometimes the dignity, courage and unconditional trust and love of an animal can have a similar transformative impact:

The stray

I grew up in a tough area and I was a tough kid. When I was ten I hooked up with a group of other kids and we called ourselves the Clan. Our mission was simple: to cause trouble. We used to break into shops and houses and steal things. We also used to hit on kids who weren't as tough as us. We also hit on stray cats and dogs. I remember one cat in particular. It was so revolting. It had only one eye, no tail and was very skinny and there were sores on his head. Life had clearly been pretty rough for this cat.

Whenever this cat came up to us hoping for food or attention one of the boys used to stub cigarettes out on his head. I was encouraged to kick and throw stones. It was 'fun'. Incredibly, however nasty or violent we were to this cat he would still come up to us. It wasn't just us that was cruel to him: everyone in our neighbourhood was. He was so unappealing. Nobody wanted him around.

One day I was walking home from school when I saw this repulsive cat lying on the side of the street. It looked like he had been kicked or attacked by a vicious dog as there was a pool of blood around him. I was morbidly curious so I leaned over to get a better look. I was sure he was dead but when I bent over I could see that he was still breathing, very gently.

I knelt down and as I did he lifted his head just the tiniest bit and looked at me. Our eyes met and it was like a bolt of light went through me. I don't know why because I didn't think this stray cat meant anything to me but I started crying, sobbing. I cradled his head in my hands and in that moment I felt so much love for this cat, I can't express it. I talked to him gently and told him I was sorry for the way I had hurt him and that his life had been so harsh. I asked for his forgiveness.

As that cat's life faded away he did the most amazing thing. He licked my fingers. He must have been in so much pain but even now he was still hoping for love and compassion. I held him close to me and could hear the faintest of purrs. This dying cat trusted me to take care of him and for that brief moment this stray cat, covered in blood and injury, was the most adorable and beautiful cat I had ever seen.

When my mum found me sitting in the road and covered in the blood of a dead cat she was furious. She scolded me as we walked home and wouldn't let me bury the cat when I asked, but later that evening I returned to give him a burial.

In the days, weeks, months and years afterwards I thought a lot about how one stray tomcat had changed my mind about so many things and taught me far more than my parents or teachers ever could. This cat may have looked repulsive on the outside but he was tender and loving on the inside. I had been repulsive on the inside and I didn't want to be like that any more.

I can honestly say – and I'm not ashamed to say – that those moments with a dying stray moggie transformed my life. I concentrated harder at school, left the Clan and am currently training to be a vet. It was only after I was able to open my heart to a dying animal that nobody cared for that good things started to happen in my life. I used to want to be popular, wealthy and cool but now I just want to be more like that stray cat.

CHAPTER 6

Dying to Live

For death begins with life's first breath and life
begins at touch of death

John Oxenham

As you've seen so far in this book, a great many healing-angel
experiences relate to the idea that life doesn't end with death. As
a society we don't talk about death or dying. It is the last taboo.
But to those who have experienced an angelic encounter or
experience death doesn't appear to be the end but rather the very
beginning of life.

I have no doubt that there is an afterlife but I'm aware that
many people, even those who want it to be true, struggle with
this idea. I'm hoping this book, and especially the true 'life in
death' stories collected together in this chapter will, if not convince you that there is an afterlife, at the very least encourage you
to keep an open mind on the subject. I also hope the stories here
will help replace the negative image of the grim reaper at the
time of death with the image of angels.

The stories in the pages that follow vary from near-death experiences to people seeing angels prior to the death of a loved one or at the actual moment of death. In other stories the spirits of departed loved ones are seen or experienced some time after the death itself – a vision that some might describe as a spirit or ghost but which many people believe to be their guardian angel. Some people simply told me that they have sensed the presence of a departed loved one. In almost all cases the experience brought a sense of comfort and healing that couldn't be found elsewhere.

Perhaps the most frequently cited explanation for angelic encounters related to the death of a loved one is that the experience is triggered by intense feelings of pain and loss. Although this 'wishful thinking' idea could go some way to explaining such encounters, it can in no way explain encounters that occur at the moment of death or before it, or encounters that occur spontaneously when the person is no longer in mourning or not even aware that a loved one has died or is dying. Also not all grieving relatives or loved ones report angelic encounters or after-death communication. Once again, logical and rational explanations can't be found for all these stories.

Modern physics tells us that everything – you, me, this book – is made up of energy. Everything in the universe is made up of vibrating strings of energy and how it vibrates defines how it manifests in the physical world. In other words we are all energy; our bodies, our minds, our thoughts and our feelings. Is it so unreasonable to think then that when we die the energy of our thoughts and feelings lives on in another dimension and this energy can interact with the living? And perhaps it is the strength of the energy between people who love each other – whether dead or alive – that makes after-death communication possible.

Like angel encounters, after-death encounters – when a person believes that the spirit of a departed loved one has returned in some way – have been reported for centuries. Angels are not strictly speaking spirits because angels have never had a physical life here on earth. They are simply pure beings of love. There are, however, strong similarities between angels and spirits and in many cases one can't be mentioned without the other. Both angels and spirits can appear in the countless different ways I have mentioned in this book, such as a voice, a vision, a magical dream or coincidence, a smell and so on, and the messages they bring are often ones of love and healing. Thus throughout this book I have referred and will continue to refer to spirits as angels.

The great adventure

The unknown is always frightening so it is only natural to fear death, but I believe, based on all I have heard and read about people who have had visions of the afterlife or near-death experiences – when their lives hung in the balance – that fear should be replaced with feelings of comfort and hope.

I'd like to begin with an experience recorded by the well-known Swiss psychologist Carl Jung (1875–1961). Jung described death as 'the great adventure' because of his own near-death experience, when he had a heart attack at the age of sixty-nine, during which he believed that he had witnessed something 'unspeakably glorious'. You can read the whole account in Jung's autobiography, *Memories, Dreams and Reflections*, but if you haven't read it, or need a brief recap, here's a taster:

It seemed to me that I was high up in space. Far below I saw the globe of the earth, bathed in a gloriously blue light. I saw the deep blue sea and the continents. Far below my feet lay Ceylon, and in the distance ahead of me the subcontinent of India. My field of vision did not include the whole earth, but its global shape was plainly distinguishable and its outlines shone with a silvery gleam through that wonderful blue light. In many places the globe seemed coloured, or spotted dark green like oxidized silver. Far away to the left lay a broad expanse – the reddish-yellow desert of Arabia; it was as though the silver of the earth had there assumed a reddish-gold hue.

Then came the Red Sea, and far, far back – as if in the upper left of a map – I could just make out a bit of the Mediterranean. My gaze was directed chiefly toward that. Everything else appeared indistinct. I could also see the snow-covered Himalayas, but in that direction it was foggy or cloudy. I did not look to the right at all. I knew that I was on the point of departing from the earth. Later I discovered how high in space one would have to be to have so extensive a view – approximately a thousand miles! The sight of the earth from this height was the most glorious thing I had ever seen.

Jung gave this description before space travel and many experts agree that it is a roughly accurate description of the earth from space. Jung goes on to explain how 'profoundly disappointed' he was when his vision ended and he was shocked back into life. The vision had been so breathtaking that, 'In reality, a good three weeks were still to pass before I could truly make up my mind to live again.'

Jung was not alone in his reluctance to come back. Many others who have also caught a glimpse of the colour and comfort of the afterlife have reported similar mixed feelings when they return to earth. Olivia, who sent me this story via email, actually wanted to return:

Let me go

In 1987 I tried to end my life. It was for a whole bunch of reasons I don't want to go into here. One evening I went from chemist to chemist to buy enough sleeping pills and downed them all with a bottle of whisky in the hostel I was staying at. If my room-mate's date had shown up I might not be alive today. It was because he stood her up that she came back early to have a good cry on her pillow. She found me lifeless on the bed instead.

My stomach was pumped and I was in intensive care for several weeks and nearly didn't make it. That first night I was brought in I had this vivid experience. I saw myself on the operating table. I was outside my body. There were three doctors in the room and two nurses. They were working silently but I could see how worried they all were. Outside the door there were no hand-wringing relatives, just my room-mate – she wasn't even a friend, as we didn't get along – looking confused and shocked.

I didn't feel anything when I looked down on my body. It was like looking at a suit or dress you didn't want to put on. I was aware of feeling totally free. I'd been in such emotional torment for so long and the relief to feel free was intense. I just watched with a sense of detachment as the doctors and nurses worked on my body.

Then I was outside the hospital, floating around the grounds and in the car park. I had this amazing sense of peace. There was no way that I was ever going back to the pain I had known on earth. At last I was free. I could feel this light coming towards me but just as I was reaching up my arms to be embraced by its warmth and comfort I was back in the operating room. Once more I was looking down at my body and my stomach being pumped.

Then I noticed two people standing on either side of me. They were watching my body on the table and unlike me they looked very sad. I had never seen either of them before but I knew they were both dead. I also knew they were sisters and that they had both died in a car accident some time ago. They looked like they were dressed in sixties-style clothing. I knew that the elder sister felt responsible because she had been driving the car. This guilt was so strong that it made it impossible for her to leave her life on earth behind. And the younger sister loved her sister so much she didn't want to go anywhere without her.

I felt concern for the sisters and asked them why they were hanging around in a hospital watching people die. I told them that they were no longer alive and that they should leave this place and go to where they were meant to be. When I spoke to them I had this amazing feeling of peace, as if I was doing the right thing for the first time in years. They both looked at me with confusion and asked me what I was doing here then because I was alive and yet I wanted to be dead. In their world I wasn't where I was meant to be either.

In an instant I knew that it was not yet my time to go and that I needed to go back, and as soon as I realized this the sisters vanished. We both returned to where we were meant to be. The next thing I remember is waking up with a very dry throat in a hospital ward. Holding my hand was my room-mate. She was fast asleep with her head resting on a magazine.

I can't describe it and I can't explain it but the warmth and love I felt for my room-mate and for everyone around me was so incredible at that moment. I was intensely, deeply grateful to be alive and all these years later that feeling has remained unchanged. I try to live each moment to the full because I know that everything we do in this life is being noticed, and whenever the living don't appreciate what they have this causes pain and confusion in the afterlife and stops spirits moving on to their destiny. I haven't seen the afterlife again but I know that when my time comes to pass over (and I hope this doesn't sound too strange) I will also feel intensely grateful to be dead.

Both Jung and Olivia's lives hung in the balance, so their remarkable journeys would probably be classified as near-death experiences. Near-death experiences tend to happen when a person is close to death or has been declared clinically dead. Such instances are surprisingly common. In one recent study, researchers quizzed 710 kidney-dialysis patients and found that, out of seventy patients who had suffered a life-threatening event, forty-five had gone through a near-death experience. And research by Virginia University shows that 10 per cent of heart-arrest patients, and 1 per cent of other cardiac patients, had reported having had a near-death experience.

Near-death experiences occur in both sexes, in every culture, and at all ages. But, in spite of considerable differences in ages, cultures and diseases, many features of near-death experiences are remarkably similar. Many report periods of personal confusion, disorientation or a void in their surroundings just as the experience begins. This is followed by a near-blinding light that is comforting and familiar. The person may feel detached from their body in some way. They may look down on it. Some see friends and relatives who have passed on and report having non-verbal communication with them. Some are shown images of places of great beauty and peace and there are feelings of love far greater than they ever experienced on earth. Many find themselves in a tunnel with a light at the end. Others hear a voice telling them that it is not their time and they need to return to their earthly body. Some may experience a life review when they see their entire life in a flashback.

Sceptics argue that near-death experiences, or NDEs, can be explained by oxygen starvation to the brain or the side effects of drugs or medication, but those who have had an NDE typically describe perfectly what happened while they were in a coma or close to death, leaving medics and scientists confounded. There will always be those who dismiss this phenomenon as nothing more than hallucination but the similarities between NDEs are so strong that they can and should be taken as 'proof' that something most definitely exists beyond our physical bodies and conscious minds. And even if one day physiological explanations provide some sort of explanation they can still never fully disprove the possibility of life after death.

Nietzsche once wrote that 'Even a thought, even a possibility, can shatter and transform us'; and reading what people have seen, heard, felt and understood from glimpses of the afterlife can be very powerful indeed because these stories truly open our minds to the possibility that this life does not end with death.

Daniel's story is a fine example of how a near-death experience can offer hope, comfort and a sense of purpose in this life and the next:

Gone today, here tomorrow

In 2005 I suffered a massive heart attack and needed a triple bypass. After the operation I had this vivid memory of having been to another time and place. At the time I didn't allow myself to believe in it because my doctor told me it was induced by the drugs I was given, but during the months of my recovery period the images I had seen kept flashing back into my head. They wouldn't let go of me and something in me didn't want to let them go.

I'll tell you what I saw before discussing the real magic behind all this. In my vision I was aware of a really bright light. Out of the light I saw an angel with the most piercing blue eyes and huge blue wings. I wasn't afraid. I just had this amazing feeling of comfort and grace. The angel held out her hand – I'm saying she because it felt like a she to me, but there was no way of knowing for sure – and I drifted or floated out of my bed. I knew I was leaving my body behind but there was no feeling of loss. I just followed the angel and she took me out of the hospital and into a field of blue grass and blue trees. There was no sound, nor any other beings around, just me and my angel. I was in a place of calm, warmth and oneness with everyone and everything.

We moved on and eventually I looked down to the world of the living and saw my children. I saw my son working at his computer and my daughter changing my granddaughter's nappy. I floated down into their world. I wanted them to know that I loved them but they didn't see or sense me. I could hear what they were thinking and feeling and their feelings and thoughts cut right through me. My death made them feel sad but didn't matter greatly to them. I didn't have a strong connection with them.

As soon as I sensed their detachment the hand that my angel had extended to me slowly and very gently started to slip away. I was floating back to the world of the living. When I reached the hospital the gentle grip was released and the next thing I remember is waking up after the operation.

In the following months my wife cared for me at home. My children tried to help all that they could but they had busy lives. I missed seeing them around and then I realized how they must have felt when they were growing up. I'd never been there. I'd been married to my job and not my family. Up until my heart attack I'd worked my way to the top but along the way I'd sacrificed so much family time I must have become something of a stranger to them. No wonder they had felt very little for me when I had had my heart attack. I couldn't allow that to continue so for the last three years I've worked really hard to regain their love and their trust.

It's not been easy but slowly and surely my children are letting me into their lives and their hearts. One of the first things I did when I felt strong enough was have an open discussion with them about the kind of father I had been. I told them that I couldn't change the past but that I wanted to be a part, however small, of their future. I told them I was sorry that I had been chasing excitement and reward at work when the real excitement and reward had been growing up before my eyes.

My near-death experience has changed me in so many ways. I'm not frightened of dying now but I am frightened of leaving life behind with missed opportunities to be there for those who need me. I seem to have developed an understanding for what really matters in life and a feeling for the hurt and concerns of others. I really want to help others with whatever concerns them and hope to do my best helping others the rest of my life.

Sally's approach to life has also changed dramatically after her near-death experience:

Vital signs

I'd just delivered my first child when I felt myself getting faint. I struggled to breathe and my doctor told me I was bleeding. I could hear my heart beating loud and fast. I was given an oxygen mask and then everything inside and outside of me stopped. It was like a freeze frame. There was no more breathing, no more heartbeat, no more hustle and bustle, just wonderful peace and calm. I felt light and spaced-out as I floated to the ceiling and left my bloated, heavy body behind.

I felt a white light all around me. It was warm and I floated like I was in a Jacuzzi. I could sense the earth breathing like it was alive. I could see a light around everything that was alive: trees, flowers, grass, animals, volcanoes and humans. I wanted to merge with the light forever, but then I looked down on my newborn baby. In an instant it felt like I was being snapped back into my body. The heartbeat started up again. It sounded so loud. I heard the breathing again. It was like stepping into a pair of slippers. I was back and when I opened my eyes I could see tubes everywhere and nurses hovering over me checking for vital signs. I stayed in hospital for the next few weeks getting my strength back.

I can honestly say my life changed forever that day and not just because I became a mother for the first time. I used to be terrified of the emptiness and darkness and loneliness of death. I've been going to church all my life but I never really believed in an afterlife. Now that I know for sure that there is light, warmth and love waiting for me when I die, I have no fear. I look forward to meeting that light again but until then I see the world and everyone and everything in it in a totally different way. I realize how fragile, vibrant and beautiful life is.

This final account of a near-death experience was sent to me by William, who was involved in a car crash:

The final curtain

I have vague memories of being strapped to a stretcher and taken to an ambulance. I remember hearing the paramedics talking to each other and the ambulance siren whirling. Next thing I remember is waking up just as we were arriving at hospital, but in between I think I died and went to heaven.

I remember this blinding light and then it vanished and all around me I saw faces that I recognized. I saw both my grandmothers and my mother. I could sense that there were many others behind them wanting to see me. My father was hugging me. He had died more than ten years ago. He'd suffered from dementia but he was clear and focused now. Everyone was so happy to see me except my old friend John, who was shaking his head. John had died only a few months ago from a sudden and unexpected heart attack. We'd known each other all our lives and it was a huge shock to me. We didn't speak but silently I asked John why he wasn't pleased to see me and he let me know it was because I needed to know my options and choose.

There was no hesitation. I chose life but not because I feared death; quite the opposite, in fact. I chose life because death was so beautiful and I wanted to bring some of that beauty I had experienced back to earth to the people I loved. I wanted to share my heaven with them. Later I told the paramedics who saved my life what I had seen. They didn't seem surprised at all. One of them told me that he hears this kind of story all the time and it's convinced him that there is an afterlife.

I've learned so many positive things from my experience. First and foremost I don't fear death. I fear losing my wife and children but I don't fear the final curtain. Also so many things that were of importance to me before just aren't. Almost everything around me now is trivial. Material stuff is just junk – it all disappears, you know, because when you pass behind that curtain it all falls away. And I don't live in fear any more. 'What if I do that?' I now know that life is really short. Each day is a gift, and I am living on borrowed time; it can end at any instant. I am now determined to live life fully and passionately, not just exist.

181

A number of researchers have attempted to describe the after effects that are often experienced by those involved and it would seem that in up to 90 per cent of cases people do report feeling more spiritual. Fear of death disappears and this results in more thoughtful, compassionate living and a childlike sense of happiness, wonder and contentment. In some cases complete reversals of personality take place. Previously unforgiving personalities become more compassionate and no longer feel the need to judge others. Overachievers are transformed into reflective thinkers, those who take others for granted have a greater appreciation for life, and those indifferent to the suffering of others become more involved members of society resolved to make an improvement in the world.

What is most remarkable, though, is that many of those who have had a near-death experience say that they have never felt more alive than when they were dead. Some go so far as to say that perhaps in death they are actually alive, in a kind of reverse understanding of existence. Maybe the most important thing they learn (and this is perhaps the most important thing such stories can teach us) is that you don't need to 'die' in order to live. There are opportunities right now, in this very present divine moment, to transform your thinking, be all that you can be and live the adventure of your life to the full.

Angel eyes

This next batch of angelic encounters all occurred close to or at the moment of a person's death. Some of these accounts are from people who were not with the person at the moment of death but were somewhere else – for example, at work or in their car. Other stories come from people who witnessed or experienced something extraordinary while in the same room as the person dying.

It doesn't surprise me that there are so many reports of people seeing angels when death is near, because perhaps nothing sharpens our spiritual awareness more than the closeness of death. As you've seen throughout this book, seeing angels is less about visions of angels with wings and halos and more about discovering the very real angel within ourselves. Perhaps when death, either our own or that of a loved one, is on the cards we feel closer than ever to our inner angel because our eyes, minds and hearts are open and receptive and we can at last see through angel eyes. This could go some way to explaining what Nathan saw the day his wife died peacefully:

The golden angel

My wife died at nine thirteen a.m. on 2 June 1999. I'd been told to expect the worst and had spent the night by her bedside holding her hand. I think she knew I was there because every so often I felt her gently, very gently, squeeze my fingers. I was emotionally and physically exhausted but I didn't dare close my eyes and let sleep take over. I wanted to be with my wife until the very end. A nurse came in and quietly placed a coffee on the table beside my bed. She didn't say anything but her smile said everything. Nurses get a lot of criticism these days but I couldn't fault the level of care and compassion my wife and I had been given since she had been diagnosed with cancer three years earlier.

I let go of my wife's hand and nodded my thanks to the nurse as she left. I started to drink my coffee and just happened to glance back at the door. When I did I became aware of what looked like two clouds drifting towards me. Each cloud was several feet high and wide and they hovered about three or four inches from the ground. I wasn't frightened at all. I just knew this was the moment my wife was going to leave me.

Gradually these two clouds enveloped the bed my wife was lying in. Even though I was sitting on the bed they did not envelop me. I looked at my wife through the mist and saw kneeling beside her on the pillow the figure of a girl. She was no more than a foot or two in height and she was dressed in white robes and glowed with a golden light that was so beautiful to behold. There was something on her head. I couldn't make out what it was but it looked like a tiara of some sort. This little figure had her hands raised over my wife's forehead. I saw my wife's face change from one of fatigue, worry and pain to one of peace and calmness.

I think I got up at this point. I fully realized what was going on and I wanted to fight it. I pushed my head into the mist and kissed my wife. She opened her eyes and smiled at me. That brief moment of connection meant the world to me because the last time we spoke had been months ago and the words between us had not been the ones I would have wanted to be the last we ever spoke to each other. I hadn't known at the time that she would collapse and enter a world of silence. Now I told my wife how much I loved her and I'm convinced I saw her nod her head slightly. And then the light went out of her eyes and I knew she had gone.

I sat back in my chair and saw what I believe to be my wife sit up, take the golden angel by the hand and step into the cloud, like a carriage awaiting her. Suddenly, the vision was gone and I was alone in the room with the body of my wife.

Not long afterwards the nurse came back in to collect my coffee cup. When I told her my wife had died she didn't believe me at first and called the doctors on duty. Attempts were made to revive her but I didn't stay to witness them. I knew my wife was not coming back. She had gone to a world of beauty, joy, peace and calm and I was happy for her. I also felt this surge of elation within me that my human eyes had been granted this vision – a vision that comforts and uplifts me whenever I miss holding and hugging the amazing woman who shared thirty-seven wonderful years with me.

Shelley's incredible experience happened on the evening of her father's death:

The force

About an hour before my father died I became aware of two spirits standing beside his bedside, on either side of it. I don't know how they got into the room or who they were. They looked like two handsome young men and both were dressed in police uniform.

The men spoke to me and told me that they had come to help my father on his journey. They said they would take good care of him. I don't know why I didn't seize the moment to ask them questions. It's hard to explain but at the time I had this overwhelming sense that everything was as it should be. It felt right and natural that these men should be here, even if I didn't know who they were.

I don't know how long I was aware of their presence but just before they appeared my father had started to get restless. He had complained of not being able to see anything because it was so dark around him but when the men appeared he seemed to know who they were immediately. He held out his right hand and both the men held on to it. He was smiling now. He looked at me and smiled even more because he knew I could see them too.

The three of them held hands for what seemed like a split second and forever at the same time. All three were smiling and the more they smiled the younger they looked. At one point it was as if they turned into boys. My brother and mother were in the room at the time. I looked at them because I wanted them to share in this but they were sobbing. I longed for them to see what I saw but I knew they could not.

Eventually the two spirits let go of my father's hand and it fell back on the bed. I heard my father sigh like someone who is settling down for a long nap and in an instant my father was what we call dead. But the smile never left his face.

The two spirits stood for a while beside my father's bedside until two spirits became three spirits. My father was still wearing his nightclothes but he looked happy, strong and full of health. It was a blessing to see him that way. I tried to get up to touch him one last time but some force was holding me back, pinning me to my seat.

My brother accused me of being cold when I didn't break down after my father's death. I considered telling him what I had seen but then I thought it would upset him that he hadn't seen it too, so I have kept quiet all these years. It is such a relief to share this with you now. I hope it gives comfort to others grieving the loss of someone they love very much.

Just one more thing you might like to know. I knew my father wasn't close to his parents but I do wonder why they weren't there instead of these young men. I got my answer when I was sorting through my father's things. I came across a photo of three boys smiling broadly in front of the camera. One was my father and the other two I recognized instantly as the boys I had seen when my father died. When I asked my mother about them she told me that when my dad was growing up these two boys had been his best friends. They had all wanted to be policemen when they grew up and, while my father did join the force, when these boys were just fifteen they had both been killed in a freak coach accident. My father had mourned the loss of their friendship all his life.

Shelley's story shows that it is not always our blood relatives who are with us at the very end; sometimes it can be other people who we for some reason or another feel more comfortable with. In the world of spirit 'family' is whoever you feel connected to. Often that will be actual family and loved ones but it can also be other people or even animals. I have read stories of people seeing their beloved pets before they die as well as stories of people being greeted by people they barely knew, but whose destiny was in some way intertwined with theirs. For example, one man emailed to say that before she died his wife spoke about a boy she had sponsored for many years with Save the Children. She'd never met that boy but had always loved reading his letters and had been very upset when he died from a serious stomach disorder at the age of thirteen.

This next story was sent to me by Natalie. It's about her son, Daniel, who was only five at the time:

Glad recognition

I was making dinner at the time and Daniel was driving me crazy as usual. He'd just come back from visiting my mum in hospital with his eldest sister so I asked him to help me lay the table. Mum had been ill for quite a while now but the doctors had told her there was reason to hope she might pull through.

Daniel kept chattering on and on but I didn't really listen until he asked me why Mum kept talking to Sammy. I think I dropped a plate or something because I had never spoken to him about Sammy. Sammy was the brother I never had. He was born two years after me but died when he was only ten days old. I asked Daniel to explain and he told me that when he had visited Mum she kept pointing to the ceiling and telling him that Sammy was up there, waiting for her. Then Daniel said he had seen him too and that he was a funny boy who liked to laugh.

At the exact moment we were talking I got a phone call from the hospital telling me that Mum had gone into cardiac arrest and was slipping away. They were doing all they could but the signs were not positive. When we got to the hospital it was too late. Mum had gone. I went in to see her and she looked like she wasn't dead, just sleeping. She had the tiniest hint of a smile and the only way I can describe her expression is one of glad expectancy or recognition. She was going to meet the son she never got a chance to know.

As mentioned previously, often young children have the ability to see through angel eyes. They haven't yet encountered the disbelief of adults. Something fairly similar happened to Tracy. Sixty-four years later she can remember very clearly the night her sister died:

Only four

My little sister, Margaret, was too good for this world. She got ill really fast and had to leave us when she was only four. I often wonder what it would have been like to have had a sister. I've got two brothers, so I can't complain, but it would have been lovely to have girly chats with a sister. I miss that. I don't worry about her, though, because I know that wherever she is she is meant to be there. I also know that she is happy and being well taken care of. I know this because I saw angels take her away the night she died.

I remember that night in every detail. For some reason I woke up. Normally I would curl back to sleep in bed but this time something made me get up. I walked on to the landing and saw the light on in my sister's room. The door was open and I saw my parents sitting on either side of her bed with one of her hands in each of theirs. I could see that they were sleeping. My sister wasn't, though. She was wide awake. She was looking at a figure standing at the end of her bed. I could only see the back of this figure but it was incredibly tall. It looked like its head touched the ceiling and its feet sank into the floor. Then I saw a bright shaft of light open up in the ceiling. In that shaft of light I saw three angels.

My sister seemed to know who they were because she smiled so fondly at them. I saw the tall figure and the three angels float towards her and lift her out of bed. They hovered for a moment as my sister looked at my mum and dad sleeping and then at me. She knew I was looking and she smiled and waved and then the image was gone. I went back to bed feeling so happy and so safe. I can't describe how good I felt.

The next morning I knew what had happened before Mum and Dad asked me to come down into the kitchen so they could tell me something. My sister had died in her sleep. As best I could with my childish vocabulary, I described what I'd seen to Mum and Dad and as I did so I could see a look of wonder in Mum's eyes.

I'm getting on a bit now and I can honestly say that in the many years I've been blessed with I have always felt that my sister was close by. I don't think of her as dead. I think of her as being in another place. I saw her leave and I saw how happy she was to go. In my heart I know she has not died and that she hasn't left me. So whenever people ask me how many brothers and sisters I have my reply is always the same, 'There are four of us: two brothers and one sister.'

Grieving relatives don't always see angels, but hearing loved ones talk about angels when they die can be just as reassuring and comforting. May didn't have 'angel eyes' when her father died but what her father told her has opened her heart and her mind to belief in angels:

Two angels, one man

Before my father died he told me he saw two angels at the foot of his bed. He said they had been there for many days and nights. When he first started speaking about them I didn't pay much attention. My father hadn't made much sense for the last two years because he was suffering from dementia. He'd never talked about angels before, though. When he first mentioned them he thought they were men. I know this because he asked me to get them both some chairs; he didn't want them to get tired. He also asked me to offer them a cup of tea or glass of water.

Every morning when I went to see Dad he would mention the angels. He seemed to really enjoy their company. I even felt a bit jealous because he made it clear he didn't enjoy mine. Every time I came in he would ask me who I was. It was heartbreaking. I'd always been a daddy's girl and we'd been very close. Even when I got married he was still the one I would turn to for advice. In many ways I already felt like I had lost him. This man wasn't the loving dad I knew.

Then one morning I came in and he knew exactly who I was. It was a miracle. The doctor said it was a miracle. For a glorious twenty minutes he was alert, lucid and loving, just as I remembered him. My dad came back. He told me how much he loved me and how much he wanted me to be happy. I told him how much I missed him. We hugged and talked. It was beautiful. Then when I had to leave to pick my children up from school he told me that he knew who the men at the bottom of his bed were now. He told me they weren't men but angels and that they had come to take him away. I left the room with tears rolling down my face because my father was starting to babble again. I didn't look back because I didn't think I could cope with him forgetting who I was again.

An hour or so later when I was walking my children home from school I got the call I had been dreading. My father had died. I didn't feel as devastated as I thought I would, though, because of that happy twenty minutes I had spent with my dad and because of what he had said about the angels taking him away.

Sandra shares a similar enlightening experience here:

Effie

My father, who died eight years ago now, suffered from cancer of the bones. After his diagnosis he started to pat his left shoulder. We would ask him if he was in pain but he would say no, and smile, and say that he had a fairy on his shoulder called Effie. Effie seemed to bring him such comfort. Effie disappeared for a few months and then reappeared a month before he died. Once again she brought him such comfort and continued to comfort him as his life ended.

After my father died I was in town with my mother when I went into a shop and this fairy figure seemed to call out to me from the shelf. I knew I had to buy her and I placed her on my father's grave where his left shoulder might be. I felt she was a comfort to him in life and I know she continues to comfort him in death.

Regardless of whether or not a grieving relative can actually witness the same visions that some dying people report, just knowing that angels are perhaps the last thing a person sees before they leave their life behind and enter the next can be incredibly comforting.

Stories of angelic encounters when a person dies are moving and astonishing, but equally astonishing are the experiences of those who were not present when a loved one died, or were not even aware that they were dying, but still had an experience at the same time. I love reading these stories because once again they show how the bonds of love will always be stronger than the physical boundaries of place, time and space.

Anita emailed me to tell me about something remarkable that happened to her when her sister died:

Two thirty-nine a.m.

I've always believed there was someone watching over me. Until I was twenty-six that person was my living sister, Melanie. She was seven years older than me and when my mum went awol she looked after me. Mercifully we weren't split up and were put in foster care together. Even after we'd grown up and got jobs we still lived a few doors away from each other. Life didn't seem right without her close by. People often joked that we were two for the price of one.

The night Melanie died I had this vision. I was tossing and turning trying to get to sleep when at the foot of my bed I saw this lady dressed in white and she was smiling at me. I couldn't see any wings but she did seem to have a halo shining above her. There was an aura about her that made me know I was in the presence of an angel or something beyond my understanding.

She kept on smiling at me as if she was bursting to tell me a wonderful secret and then she turned clockwise three times and on the third time she turned around my sister was standing beside her, holding her hand. My sister looked so happy I felt happy for her. Before they vanished they both pointed at the clock by my bedside; it read two thirty-nine.

It was almost like a dream in that I have no idea when she left. It was as if she was there one moment and in a heartbeat she was gone. I have no explanation, though I know I wasn't dreaming. I fell into a deep sleep.

I woke up a couple of hours later. My phone was ringing. It was Nigel, Melanie's boyfriend, and he was sobbing. He told me that there had been an accident. The two of them had been out late to a party. When they walked home a motorcycle had mounted the pavement and knocked Melanie out. She was rushed to hospital but the doctors couldn't save her. Melanie was dead.

My first reaction was shock and then the image of my dream came into my head. I asked Nigel what time Melanie had died. He said he wasn't sure. In a daze I threw some clothes on and went to the hospital. On the journey there I didn't shed a tear. I don't think it had really sunk in that my sister, the better half of me, had died. When I got to the hospital the staff must have found my behaviour very bizarre. Apparently I just kept asking over and over again what time Melanie had died. Nobody knew for sure until a doctor sat down with me. It was only when he told me that she had been declared dead at two thirty-nine a.m. that the tears started to flow.

My sister died fifteen years ago now. I still miss her every second of every day but I know what I saw that night. I saw an angel. I saw my sister. At the exact moment she died she had wanted to be with me, just as I would have wanted to be with her. We are still together in spirit and always will be.

Jenna sent me this breathtaking story:

Pink slippers

My mother died peacefully in her sleep at the magnificent age of ninety-eight. I wasn't with her when she died but I believe she was with me. It was about four in the afternoon and I was getting ready to visit her in her residential home. I stopped at a shop to buy her some of her favourite scented tissues, for which she had developed a passion during the past few years, but sadly there were no boxes left.

I drove up to the home and parked my car. When I got out I saw something I shall never forget. I saw my mum walking towards me. She was in her dressing gown and she had her pink slippers on. She hadn't walked for years. I was lost for words. She came up to me and told me not to worry about the tissues because she didn't need them any more. I just kept on staring at her. I could not believe what I was seeing. I opened and shut my eyes and she was still there.

Another car drew up behind me and I lost my concentration briefly as I shut my door. When I looked up I saw mum's dressing gown disappear back into the nursing-home entrance. I ran after her and when I got inside I asked the receptionist if they had seen which way she had gone. The receptionist shook her head so I went into the common area. I couldn't see her anywhere. I came back out in the hall and a nurse came up to me. She looked troubled and asked me to come into a private area.

I started to chatter away about mum's remarkable recovery but the nurse looked even more puzzled. She called for a doctor and then I heard the news. My mum had actually died twenty or so minutes ago. She had already been dead, then, when I was hunting for her tissues. She had already been dead when I saw her in the car park.

A cup of tea was pressed in my hand and I was asked if I wanted to see her body. Shocked to the core, I nodded. They asked me about what I had seen but I told them I must have been mistaken. When I went upstairs and saw Mum she was wearing the same dressing gown and slippers she had been wearing in my vision. Neatly stacked on the floor beside her were several boxes of her tissues.

I know what I saw but I haven't told anyone. My husband and sons think I'm crazy enough anyway and I don't want them to worry about me because they know how tight Mum and I were. I don't know what I think now. Did I imagine it? But then how did I know what she would be wearing? She had a number of dressing gowns and about ten pairs of slippers, all in different colours. How did I know she would be wearing her pink ones?

The experience has mystified me and sent chills up my spine but it has also been very comforting. I've always believed in life after death and my belief is stronger than ever now. I know that wherever Mum is she's still alive, because she is alive in my memories and in my heart.

A number of people have written to me to say that a clock stopped at the precise moment a loved one died. Tari was one of those people. Here's her story:

Stop watch

About thirteen years ago my grandmother had her third and final heart attack. The whole family except me and my brother went to see her in hospital. I was only ten years old at the time and I think my mother thought it might be too much so she asked her best friend, Aunt Sally – she wasn't my aunt but I always called her that – to look after us both at home.

I liked it when Aunt Sally looked after us because we got to eat chocolate and watch TV. I was looking forward to watching this one show in particular and kept checking my watch to see how much longer I had to wait. After half an hour or so of checking I realized that my wristwatch had stopped so I checked the oven clock. It had also stopped at the same time, seven fifteen, and so had the clock on the mantelpiece. This felt a little spooky to me as the TV had been working constantly and I wondered if my grandmother had died and had come to the house to let me know.

Not long after – I think it was about nine p.m. – Mum called from the hospital to let me know that Grandmother had died. Everybody was upset and so I forgot about the clock-watching for a few days, but when I did finally ask Mum what time Grandmother had died she said it was at around seven p.m. The time had been seven fifteen at home when my wristwatch, the oven clock and mantelpiece clock all stopped, so perhaps Grandmother had lingered in the hospital to comfort Mum before visiting me.

You can call this coincidence but it doesn't seem like that to me. The clocks all told the right time the morning after, without me winding them up or replacing batteries.

Tari asked me if I knew of other people this had happened to and I told her that I certainly did. I also told her that, although I had never experienced the phenomenon myself, my mother taught me the 'Grandfather's Clock' song when I was little, some forty years ago, and I'd always believed that the words might be true. I also believe that this clock stopping is a sign from the world of spirit, a message that when we die the concept of time disappears and only love, warmth and light remain.

Another after-death experience which is not uncommon involves smells. Suddenly one becomes aware of a familiar scent, maybe perfume or shampoo. As Sam discovered, scents can be a way for loved ones to let us know they are nearby:

Scent of a woman

My girlfriend always used to wear Chanel No. 5. It was her favourite perfume. When she was diagnosed with cancer she stopped wearing perfume. She started to smell of medication and hospitals. I missed many things about her when she faded away before my eyes. I missed her laugh, her hugs, her energy and the smell of her perfume.

After she died I couldn't bear going back home so I stayed in my brother's flat. Ever since she'd got ill I had carried around this beautiful photograph of her. I'd taken it about a year previously. When I got to my brother's the first thing I did was place it standing up on a chair beside the sofa-bed I was going to sleep on. The day had been exhausting so, after chatting for a while with my brother, we both decided to turn in. My brother went to his room and I was left alone.

I remember just sitting on the sofa-bed feeling numb. I missed her but I was also glad her suffering was over. I didn't feel her around me, as people often say they do when someone dies, and wondered if that was my fault. Perhaps her illness had put a distance between us. I felt guilty that I missed the happy, healthy her and not the ill and exhausted woman she became. I beat myself up a lot about this. I felt guilty and depressed that a part of me was relieved that I didn't have to see her suffering any more.

I got ready for bed and then I got this huge whiff of Chanel No. 5. Then it was gone. I backed up and retraced my steps and then the smell hit me again. I started to sniff around the room. After a few moments, I found myself standing next to the sofa-bed because this was definitely where the scent was coming from. I found myself staring at the picture of my laughing girlfriend.

It was an awesome experience. It wasn't imagination. It was real. The next morning the smell had gone but my memory of it hadn't. I wasn't imagining it. I think this was my girlfriend's way of telling me to remember the happy times we shared and to stop focusing so much on what was sad. She had forgiven me. She wanted me to know that she loved me and that, even though I pulled away, she understood and still shared a loving connection with me. Her unconditional love has touched my heart in ways I can't explain.

Love doesn't die. People who love us will often come back to comfort us, heal our pain or offer forgiveness, and to let us know that they are still with us and always will be.

It's been my experience that the spirit of a departed loved one will tend to show itself in a way that you will understand, in a way that will speak directly to you, without causing panic or alarm. For Sam it was through scent, his girlfriend's favourite perfume, but there are so many other ways. Some of the subtler (and thus more common) ways in which spirits will try to connect with us involve visiting us in our dreams, sending feelings of love and comfort, and planting thoughts and memories of themselves in our minds. They may also speak through other people, without those people realizing that they are being a channel for spirit. For example, if you are grieving for your husband and you meet someone and hear that person saying something that your husband always used to say, your husband in spirit may be using that person as an unconscious medium to let you know he is still around you.

Sometimes spirits may reach out to us in a physical way: we

may see something out of the corner of our eyes, smell something when no one else does, feel like the hair is standing up on
the back of our necks or like the temperature around us has
shifted, etc. Then there are those signs we can actually see, hear
or touch, such as lights flickering or phones ringing or the
appearance of meaningful signs at significant moments.

These are just a few of the many ways in which the dead can
'talk' to us. For each person it will be different and may often
occur in the way we least expect. I had hoped for visions and
spectacular signs immediately after the death of my mother but
it was several years later, through dreams and a still inner voice,
that I met her once again and was reassured of her eternal love.
Therefore my advice to anyone who longs to receive a sign from
a departed loved one is to be patient, because if you listen with
your heart the answers and the longed-for reunion will come.
This is exactly what Denise did and here's her story:

Byzantine

I would like to share with you an experience I had recently. I have
always been open to the possibility that there is life after death, particularly since my father died recently. I had been reading a book by a
famous American medium and sent a mental note to my dad asking
him to send me a sign, but nothing came.

Then a while later, in the middle of the night – I'm sure I was
asleep – I heard a voice say only one word: Byzantine. It was so powerful it made me sit up in bed and repeat the word several times, so I
wouldn't forget it. The next morning I wrote the word down on a

notepad, and all morning wondered what it could mean as I had never heard it before.

Foolishly, I at first thought it was a sign that I should enter in the lottery using the letters converted into numbers according to their order in the alphabet, B being 2 and Y being 25, etc. Of course, I didn't win and I resigned myself to the fact that I would probably never know what the experience had meant.

Two days later I was watching a gardening programme on the TV. I had previously recorded it in case I missed it. The gardener on the TV was describing a plant which is covered in silver-grey hairs. Its name was *stachys byzantina*.

I knew then that this was the sign I had been waiting and hoping for; not only in terms of the name but also the fact that my dad had the most beautiful head of silver-grey hair. I still have the programme on video and feel so close to my dad when I watch it.

Mandy, whose story is below, believes that her husband in spirit found a very special way to speak to her family.

Angel bird

My husband always used to call me his angel and when we had my daughter Poppy he called her angel bird, because she had such a tiny appetite and ate like a bird. My husband adored Poppy. In fact he adored children. There was so much love in our family and I refused to believe it could end when he died in 2006 from prostate cancer. I still sensed him all around me. It was different for his mum, though.

I'd call in on my mum-in-law every day after work to have a chat and make sure she was eating okay. She seemed to hardly eat at all. Sometimes she'd go for days with just a scone for sustenance. I'd bring food along but she hardly touched it. It broke my heart to see her like this. She used to be so vibrant and alive. One day, in yet another attempt to get her to eat, I decided that we should all eat in the garden as it was a lovely, sunny day. I brought my daughter Poppy along. She loved playing in her grandparents' garden – it was much bigger than ours.

Something very special happened that afternoon. I was sitting with my husband's mum on the patio watching Poppy play when this little wild bird flew down beside Poppy and let her pet it for at least a minute. I got up, curious to see if it would let me pet it too, but it flew away. I sat down again and the bird reappeared and allowed Poppy to pet it yet again.

It was extraordinary but even more extraordinary was my mum-in-law's reaction. She looked at me and told me it was her son, my husband, saying goodbye to us and his daughter, his angel bird. How often does a wild bird let a child pet it without flying away? The bird wasn't injured and my daughter wasn't throwing breadcrumbs down. From that day on my mum-in-law got some of her spirit back. She died two years later but she died with a smile on her face because she knew her son was waiting for her.

Healing stories like this show once again how the line between coincidence and small miracles can be very, very thin. As we've seen earlier, messages from beyond that offer hope and healing can come through animals or the world of nature. They can also come through the words of a child, as Linda discovered. Here's an extract from her letter to me:

Pretty lady

My sister Jackie was a very poorly lady, and had been for a number of years. She could never have children of her own, which left her devastated, but she adored all her nephews and nieces. Anyway, my daughter gave birth to a little girl, who she called Alix, on 1 November 2001. Because of my sister's ill health she told me that she could not go to see the baby but that she would as soon as she felt better.

On 2 March 2002 my sister suddenly died at the age of forty. She never got to see baby Alix. Then one day, when Alix was about thirteen months old, she was in her high chair in the kitchen with my husband and me having lunch (we were babysitting), and she could not stop staring at the ceiling. When we asked what she was looking at she said, 'Look, Daddad' – she couldn't say 'Granddad' – 'look at the pretty lady dancing!' And she kept saying that the lady was smiling and waving at her. We couldn't see anything.

Then, about three months later, when my daughter and I took Alix to town one day we got her a few sweets in a bag, which she held in her little hand. Suddenly she started saying, 'No, they my sweeties.' When we asked her who she was talking to she said, 'The pretty lady wants her sweets.'

I forgot to say that I had put a large picture of Alix in my sister's coffin and I'd like to think that it was my sister who Alix saw, and that she had come to see her as she had said she would.

There are many stories like this of children, especially young children, seeing things – too many for adults to dismiss them all as imagination. Children, because they are fresh from heaven and don't tend to have the level of fear and distrust that adults tend to acquire, can often see through 'angel eyes'. Instead of distrusting them or dismissing what they see or hear, we should listen to them and encourage them to believe in their own creativity and their own spirituality.

For Joanne the reassurance she needed didn't come from a child, or an animal or any physical sign. It came in a dream:

Always with me

I wanted to share with you an experience that I had a few years ago now. Like yours, my mum passed away when I was young, in fact it was when I was twenty-one. I was totally devastated and heartbroken. I was angry for a long time and did not understand why she had been taken from us. My whole family was so shocked and saddened. I also suffered from depression – which I still do, but it is managed with antidepressants.

Anyway, I longed for a sign that my mum was still here with me. I even went to a couple of psychics, but was not so sure of what they told me; some things were true but they were also so vague. I was asked to be a bridesmaid at my cousin's wedding about four years after my mum's death. This cousin was the daughter of my biological dad's sister (he died when I was about eight months old – he had depression and committed suicide).

The night before the wedding I stayed at my dad's house (he is really my stepdad but I call him Dad) and I slept in the room that used to be mine when I still lived at home with Mum and Dad. I had the most amazing dream. I dreamed that I was with a friend in my old room and we were sitting chatting on the bed. Suddenly, the lights flickered and there was my mum, sitting right next to me on my bed. She took hold of my hands and told me that she loved me. I told her that I loved her too. She smiled and gave me a hug, then she disappeared and I woke up. I was a bit surprised at having this dream. It seemed to be so real. I could actually remember feeling her hands in mine. I have been convinced ever since that she is always with me.

Janice felt her mother's presence in a different but equally reassuring way:

Loud and clear

On 4 July 2007 my mother died from complications related to what should have been routine gall-bladder surgery. I didn't expect my mum to die, even though she got sick and was in hospital for five months. I wasn't with her when she died and when I heard the news I remember feeling this urgent need to get some fresh air. I was at home and stepped outside on to my porch. As soon as I was outside I felt my mother all around me as if she was standing in front of me. It's so hard to describe but I just knew she was there.

I looked up and saw the wind chime my mum had given me as a housewarming present. It was a warm day and there was very little breeze but something inside me asked my mum to ring the chime for me. All of a sudden the chime started to ring, loud and clear. It rang like that, without any breeze to make it ring, for about thirty seconds and then it stopped. It was a beautiful experience and a gift that helped begin to heal my tremendous grief.

Earlier in the book we discussed physical or tangible signs, like white feathers, clouds or wind chimes, as in the story above, that angels can sometimes use to alert us to their presence. Many of these signs are also ones that people believe can signal the presence of lost loved ones. This brings me back to the confusion that some people have between what a spirit is and what an angel is, especially as many people talk about after-death communication as angelic encounters. Although there may be subtle differences, in that angels have never been earthbound, it seems to me that there may in fact be very little difference and that the concept of spirits and angels become merged whenever people feel the presence of otherworldly goodness, love and healing. This is certainly how it felt for Hannah, who shares her heartbreaking but also heart-warming story below:

Eyes wide shut

We kept hoping she'd beat it but cancer took my mum away from me when I was thirteen. I held her hand and told her I loved her and moments later she slipped away. My mum and I had always been very close. We loved all the same things and I felt as if I could tell her anything. Even when she was very ill she still wanted to know everything I was doing. She still gave me advice, even if I didn't follow it. She still nagged me to do my homework and wear longer skirts.

You can imagine how deeply I missed my mum when she was gone. I went to live with my aunt and her three children and it was a disaster from the start. My aunt had her own set of rules and her own way of mothering and it was so different to my mum's I felt completely isolated. There were so many rows and tears. After about two months I tried to run away but not having any money meant I didn't get very far.

Looking back I can see that the problem wasn't my aunt. It was my grief. I didn't know what to do with it and I took it out on the very people who were trying to be there for me. I made it very hard for them. Mercifully, I did come to my senses and I have my mum to thank for that.

My mum visited me one night about three months after she died. It was about four o'clock in the morning. I woke up and felt her presence in the room. I didn't see her but I could feel her. It was like she was sitting on the end of my bed. I tried to sit up but I couldn't move or do anything because it felt like my body was still sleeping. My eyes were closed but I could see everything. I could hear everything too. I heard my mum's voice and she told me that she would always love me and always be there for me. Then her voice disappeared and I heard what sounded like beating wings.

I kept trying to open my eyes. I wanted to see more clearly but I couldn't. You might think I was dreaming but I can tell you I was awake. I could see with my eyes closed. Eventually I was able to open my eyes and everything looked the same as usual. Even though I couldn't get to sleep I had this incredible sense of peace.

Never a day goes by when I don't miss my mum but that visit to me changed everything. I felt better because I knew she was there for me and always would be and one day I would be with her again. I would be lying if I said it was all plain sailing from then on. There were a few more arguments with my aunt but nothing as bad as before. I was finally able to let other people in and accept love from someone other than my mum and, you know what, all these years later – twenty-two, to be precise – I can actually see and feel my mum in my aunt's eyes.

Spirits often try to reach us through the language of emotion. This is why we may feel a wash of love and comfort when a spirit is reaching out to us. There are no words for that sort of feeling, but to those who have experienced it, as Hannah did and as Libby, who tells her story next, did, it can be life-changing.

Still with me

My son, Michael, was killed in a boating accident. He was just nine years old. For two years after his death I struggled with feelings of anger, guilt and pain. I could not understand why he was taken away so young. I couldn't see a way forward for me. I wanted to believe in an afterlife but I couldn't feel his presence at all. In fact the idea of an afterlife sometimes made it worse. I wondered if he was missing me or if anyone was looking after him. I remembered how he hated being on his own or sleeping without his night light on. How would he cope in a world of darkness? If it had not been for my three other children I would have seen no reason to go on. I would have willingly taken my own life to join him, wherever he was. And then on the second anniversary of his death things began to change for me.

I had just dropped my kids off at school and was walking home when this dog, a Border collie, came running up to me wagging its tail. Instantly it made me think of Michael. Of all my kids he had been the one who really wanted a pet. He'd wanted a Border collie and had already decided on a name, Marcus. Just before he died I'd seriously been considering the possibility of getting a dog for him as a surprise at Christmas. I didn't think I could cope with a Border collie, as they are so active and intelligent, so I might have gone for a quieter breed, but all the same I was probably going to get him the dog he longed for.

Suddenly, as I patted this dog's head, I felt this wave of love and warmth through my body. It started in my chest and spread outwards. By now the owner had come up and I stopped breathing for a while when he apologized for Marcus, his dog, being so friendly. It was all too much for me. Here I was on the anniversary of my son's death, patting a Border collie called Marcus, the same name I know my son would have given the dog I would have got him.

The owner must have thought I was a bit crazy because I started crying. He was an elderly man and, rare for people these days, didn't seem to be in a rush. He asked me if I was okay and I blurted out the whole story about Michael dying and how he always wanted to have a Border collie called Marcus. Then this guy said something that sent shivers down my spine. He said that perhaps it was Michael's way of telling me he was still close with me.

When trying to speak of how what this guy said made me feel, I have come to realize that it is almost impossible to do. Since then I have had so many experiences or perceptions that have touched my heart and made me feel that Michael is still with me. Sometimes these impressions come through the same smile on another child's face or one of my other children looking at me in exactly the same way Michael used to. Other times I swear I can hear Michael's voice amid the screams and shouting of his siblings.

I've also had dreams about Michael. In his dream he is always with a Border collie. Sometimes he hugs me tightly in my dreams; other times I just watch him play with his dog. I have had so many of these wonderful signs over the years. They are so subtle and fragile and when I was still raw with grief soon after his death I probably wasn't able to pick them up or notice them, but now they give me such comfort in my grief.

I'm the first to admit that these experiences are not especially meaningful or dramatic when I relate them to others. I'm also aware that many people will say I imagine them. I wish I could explain them better or make them more impressive to others, but perhaps I can't because they are not intended for others. They are intended for me and me alone, to give me comfort while I am temporarily parted from my son.

The signs Michael sends me are subtle and gentle and probably cannot ever be properly communicated or proved to others. But I am in no doubt whatsoever that Michael is close by and that the messages he sends me are all the proof I will ever need that love is stronger than death.

Each time I read Libby's story my eyes fill with tears. Out of her tremendous grief and pain, faith and goodness have emerged. There can be nothing more heartbreaking than the loss of a child. Children have so many gifts to bring the world and when they are taken before their time it can feel unnatural and cruel; but children can offer their gifts both in body and in spirit. Whether it is their passionate approach to life or their departure from this life that offers those they leave behind a greater awareness of love, children can point humanity in a direction for a more intuitive and open-minded approach to life.

There are some children who touch our lives for only a short time before they return to spirit to continue their work. These children in spirit teach us to reach into the world of spirit so we can recognize and remember that we are much more than our physical bodies. We are all living spiritual beings. Children in spirit want us to find our spiritual roots. They want to reach out to us and support us and will find ways to do so.

As Libby's story shows, wondering if a departed loved one is still suffering or is afraid or lonely can haunt our days and nights. Messages from beyond can soothe these distressing concerns with the joyful news of ongoing life. Not only is a lost loved one not suffering, but he or she is also living in happiness and freedom and in beauty beyond human understanding. In the afterlife there is no loneliness or fear.

Moving beyond grief

As we've seen, there are so many ways in which those who have passed on are seemingly able to reach back into the physical world. Each visitation bears a message of hope, reassurance, healing or just a simple signal that says, 'I'm here. I haven't left you. I'm watching over you and my love for you continues.'

Judging by the number of letters and emails I receive and the research I have done, after-death communication is definitely one of the most common spiritual experiences that people report. Some studies show that as many as three quarters of grieving parents or spouses have felt a sense of presence of the 'dead'. Sadly, many of these experiences are dismissed as coincidence or explained away as grief-induced wishful thinking, but this is unfortunate because ignoring or dismissing visitations from the other side can limit a person's potential to move beyond grief and heal.

When someone you love or care deeply about dies you can't physically touch or laugh or cry with them any more and the pain of this loss can feel unbearable. However, if you learn to experience them in a new way they can stay alive in your heart and mind, and in the belief that in the world of spirit they are with you forever.

Speaking from personal experience I know that the loss of someone you love can be one of the hardest things to face in life. A wave of grief, hurt and pain overwhelms you and life seems impossible to face without them. And you may also feel guilt because you have not said or done what you wanted to do before that person died, or were not there when they passed over.

To move beyond this sense of crisis and unbearable grief you may feel, as I did and as many of the people who submitted stories for this chapter did, that healing and moving forward is impossible. As hard and as unjust as it may seem there is no easy way to move beyond grief. I'm no bereavement counsellor but one thing I do know is that before you can move on and accept the loss you need to first experience and acknowledge your sense of loss, and this will take time. Some people take several months or years, while others are able to move through the grieving process more quickly. I also know that there are several stages to grief and you can expect to move from denial and shock and emotional numbness to overwhelming feelings of helplessness, anger, guilt, fear, desperation and emptiness.

It is so important to talk and to get one's pain moving through expression. Talking to family or friends or a support group is vital and a wonderful way to engage with others who may also understand and share similar grief. It is also important to take care of our bodies, by eating, sleeping and exercising, even if this is the last thing we want to do.

Whatever stage of the grieving process you are in, there will be pain, even for those who believe in an afterlife, because you are missing the way things used to be. This pain will come in waves and vary in intensity, like the ebb and flow of the ocean, but believe me: the pain will gradually diminish and you can learn to experience lost loved ones in a new way when you understand that each time you call on them with your heart they will hear you loud and clear.

After all I have read, seen and experienced for myself I have no doubt that every time you think about a lost loved one they are living on inside you. Remember, though, that just as you have a life and work to do in this life the spirits of the departed also have their spiritual work to do. If you keep on obsessing about them neither you nor they will be able to adjust to their new life in spirit. This doesn't mean you shouldn't think about them – that would be terrible because it would cause both you and them pain – it just means don't forget you have a life to lead here on earth, a destiny to fulfil. Remember that the greatest love and the most powerful and healing love is the love that lets a spirit free.

Just the beginning

Talking about the prospect of death, either our own or that of someone we love, is something many of us find very hard to do, but everything I have learned or experienced during the years I've spent as a paranormal researcher and writer has encouraged me to believe wholeheartedly that death is not the end. It is simply the next stage in our existence and a stage we have been preparing for the whole of our lives. Think about it: we start dying the minute we are born and each night when we sleep we travel to the world of spirit in our dreams. Seen in this light, we are all dying to live and living to die every day of our lives.

Regretfully, because death is something we do not fully understand and for which none of us feels prepared, it is something that many of us are terrified of. If we could only entertain the idea that it is not an end but rather a whole new beginning, for both ourselves and those we have loved and lost, then death really could lose its brutal sting.

I sincerely hope that this chapter has shown you that death is a natural phase in your existence and not something you should fear. Sometimes life can hurt, especially when you lose someone you love, but knowing that your loved one never really dies, and instead lives on within and all around you, can make it so much easier to bear. As I said earlier, when my mother died I was never able to sense her presence when I visited her grave, on anniversaries or even in the places we used to spend time together. I sensed it in the most unexpected moments and places. She came back to me in so many different and wonderful ways. I want to include this well-known but always remarkable bereavement poem by Mary Frye because it has touched and comforted so many grieving relatives over the decades, and because it says so eloquently and simply what I am struggling to say here:

> Do not stand at my grave and weep,
> I am not there, I do not sleep.
> I am in a thousand winds that blow,
> I am the softly falling snow.
> I am the gentle showers of rain,
> I am the fields of ripening grain.
> I am in the morning hush,
> I am in the graceful rush
> Of beautiful birds in circling flight,
> I am the starshine of the night.
> I am in the flowers that bloom,
> I am in a quiet room.
> I am in the birds that sing,
> I am in each lovely thing.
> Do not stand at my grave and cry,
> I am not there. I do not die.
>
> Mary Frye, 1932

Even when you feel abandoned and lonely, angels and the spirits of lost loved ones are all around you, waiting for you to remember and recognize them. Some people sense the presence of angels in the natural world or in the unconditional love of animals or in the faces of their children or in times of quiet memories and reflection. It doesn't matter where or how you sense their presence: just never forget that angels can be found whenever spirits are lifted by love, laughter, creativity and courage.

If you can just open your eyes and your heart and look for the goodness and love that exists within you and all around you, rest assured that you will begin to encounter angels in your own life. You will also be helping others to discover the goodness and love that lives forever within them. In this way you will be doing all you can to draw the angels close to earth so that, when the time comes for you to leave your physical body behind, not only will you have left the world a better place but you will also be flying (who knows, perhaps even soaring) without fear and guilt towards the place where angels sing – a place some like to call heaven.

CHAPTER 7

Angel Healing

Healing takes courage, and we all have
courage, even if we have to dig a little to find
it

Tori Amos

Angels are around us and deep within us. Their purpose is to heal
us by helping us to shed the burdens of fear and guilt so that feelings of unworthiness can be replaced with joy as we gently enter
a world of love. They can heal all aspects of our lives if we allow
them to – and 'allow' is the key word here. Everyone, whatever
their age or belief system, has the ability to connect with their
angels; but, because we have free will, in order for angels to help
us we need to open ourselves up to their love and healing first.
In rare cases angels can intervene directly but in most cases they
can only stand by and watch and wait for us to call out to them.

Many people think they are not special or psychic enough to
communicate with angels, that they are not chosen by them, but
this couldn't be further from the truth. Everyone is chosen and

everyone can call on their angels. The problem is that few of us find the courage to believe in the impossible, to look outside the norm that society has dictated. Far too many of us settle for an ordinary life, forgetting that it can and should be extraordinary. Far too many of us try to go it alone, without any belief in our own greatness and potential. Calling on angels for help and guidance and then listening to what they have to say is the turning point that opens up the very real possibility of healing miracles manifesting in our lives. And once we are open and receptive to the possibility of angels the real magic can begin, from the inside out.

From the inside out

In many of the stories in this book you have probably picked up on a constant theme – the theme of healing from the inside out. This makes perfect sense to me because I believe the essence of healing to be the restoration of wholeness. For true healing to occur it must be on all levels – physical, emotional and spiritual – and it must begin from the inside out.

When true healing begins the first thing you may experience is not a lessening of physical symptoms but an inner shift or a breakthrough that creates feelings of movement and energy again. Suddenly it becomes clear that you are on a new path. Whether you are recovering from a bad cold, overcoming a bout of depression or coping with the loss of a loved one, this awareness can fill your whole body, mind and spirit with feelings of relief, gratitude and joy. Listen to and connect to those feelings – the voice of your inner angel reaching out to you – because this is where true healing from the inside out begins.

I'd like to briefly bring in another of my own experiences here because, although I was too young to understand fully at the time, looking back I can see that it is a good example of angel healing from the inside out. It happened a long time ago, when I was in my teens, but I can't forget it.

Lighting the way

During my teens angels were not in my heart or mind; the only thing in my life was my eating disorder. When I look back I can't believe how I let something so dark and negative take over my life. For several years my only focus was food. My parents were not getting on and I thought it was my fault. I felt I was unworthy because I didn't appear to have any talents. I felt that I didn't deserve to eat and that taking control of my food would help me take control of my life. In a weird way it became the only positive thing about my life. If I ate only what I had planned to eat on any given day I had succeeded. If I failed, a voice in my head told me how bad and weak I was.

One morning I woke up feeling weary. As soon as I opened my eyes the destructive voice of anorexia told me that I could only eat one apple today and nothing else and that I needed to add one more hour to my exercise routine. For five days I'd been living on apples and black coffee and Diet Coke and exercising for three hours a day. This was my life now. The voice would tell me what to do and I would do it.

My head hurt as I got out of bed. Everything hurt but I had to obey the voice. I could feel my hip bones jutting out and that reassured me. I looked around for my scales – another morning ritual – but couldn't see them. I also noticed that I had forgotten to close my curtains the evening before and the window was wide open. Mentally I gave myself a kicking. I never forgot to close my curtains and my window was always closed. It was important to follow my routines. I was a bad person if I didn't. My windows were never left open because fresh air and sunlight were starting to make me uncomfortable. I also suffered from hay fever. I wondered for a moment if my mum had opened the window but then I remembered she was staying with friends that evening.

There was no getting away from it. I had to close the curtain. I had to find my scales. I shuffled across to the window, shielding my eyes from the morning sunlight. When I got there I tried to lift my arms to draw the curtains. I couldn't. My arms wouldn't move. I was stuck there. I tried again but it felt as if someone was gently holding them by my side. I tried to close my eyes but they wouldn't let me. I tried to sit back on my bed but my feet were rooted to the spot.

For several minutes I struggled but eventually I stopped fighting and just stood there and let the sunshine wrap itself around me. Then as the warmth hit my face it was as if a light bulb went on inside me. It suddenly became obvious to me that I was heading down a very dangerous road, a road that might end in my death. The voice of anorexia tried to assert itself but I shut it off. I didn't want to hear it again.

Although in that instant I made the decision to live, my recovery wasn't instant. It was a good two years before I could say that I had completely recovered. But from the moment when I made the decision to live my recovery truly began and mealtimes were no longer a battleground. My mum told me that she believed an angel had drawn my curtains back, opened my window and wrapped its arms around me that morning to stop me moving. I wasn't entirely convinced. Perhaps it was food deprivation that had made me too weak to lift my arms and I had just forgotten to draw my curtains the night before. I couldn't believe that I was special or psychic enough for the angels to care about me. But even though self-doubt stopped me embracing the full wonder of the experience, somehow after standing in the sunlight that morning my energy for life and my common sense returned. There was no longer any room inside my head for the voice of anorexia. I didn't want to listen to it any more. A softer, gentler, calmer and more loving voice had replaced it and this voice was giving me permission to live.

There was a lot of work to do in the years ahead in terms of building my self-awareness and self-esteem, but I believe my spiritual journey truly began the day I stood by my window in the sunshine. I did not realize it at the time but my inner angel and the innate spirituality I had lost faith in were making themselves heard.

Another story I'd like to place here, because it strongly focuses on healing from the inside out, was sent to me by Rachel several years ago:

Angel in my room

My addiction to the internet started really when I was being bullied at work by my boss. She hadn't liked me from the start and over time it got so bad that I couldn't sleep properly. She was very clever. It was very hard to prove that she was bullying me because she only did it when we were alone. I should have fought back but I've never had great self-esteem.

I lost what little confidence I had and for a year my life was just work and home. I never went out. I couldn't talk to my husband and my only source of comfort was the internet. I started to log on to various chat rooms and would spend hours having conversations with people I didn't know. I created a whole new life for myself. In my cyber world I was a high-powered businesswoman, not a put-upon PA. I told my husband that I was bringing work home from the office but this wasn't the truth. I was online as soon as I got home and often late into the night because I was addicted to chat rooms.

I'm not a drinker or a smoker and I don't gamble so I had no idea what was happening to me and how my addiction was eating up my life and my marriage. I would go to bed and wait until I heard my husband snoring and then tiptoe out of the bedroom to feed my addiction. Sometimes when I was slipping out like this I realized that I needed help, but my compulsion to go online was stronger than I was. It was controlling me. I couldn't escape from it.

Then the weirdest thing happened to me at work one day. My boss was out for the morning so instead of working I logged on to a chat room. I got a thrill of excitement, as this was the first time I had done this at work. It felt like an act of rebellion. After a few minutes I got this sensation that someone was looking at me. I froze with fear at first and hastily switched off the screen, thinking my boss had returned, but when I turned around there was no one there. Feeling relieved I restarted my online conversation. The topic soon drifted towards sex and I got the same feeling again. This time the hairs on my neck stood on end. It was as if someone was watching me. I jumped out of my seat and shut down my computer and as soon as I did I felt a warmth come over me. I also smelled a lovely smell; it reminded me of lavender. In that instant I knew there was an angel in my room. I felt ashamed that they had been watching me.

My eyes filled with tears and I sat there for a long time. My boss came in and I could tell she was shocked to see me like this. I mean, I was sobbing out loud. She must have thought it was because of her treatment of me, and that there might be repercussions for her if I accused her of bullying, because she couldn't do enough to help me. She offered to make me a cup of tea or drive me home.

After that day my boss never bullied me again. I think she realized she could only push me so far. What I didn't know until a few weeks later is that she had been out of the office because she had been at a disciplinary hearing – other people had complained about her and she had been given a warning. If I spoke up as well she would have been finished. She needed me to like her.

It wasn't just my work situation that improved, though: it was my life. The sensation of being watched by my angel had given me clarity about the way I was leading my life, spending hours and hours online. I discovered the courage to make changes. I told my husband that I had been lying to him and that I had been addicted to the internet. I removed the computer from my home to stop myself slipping back and I signed up for counselling via my doctor.

This all happened five years ago and I have never looked back. My boss moved on. I got a promotion at work and am now pregnant with what I hope will be the first of many children. What is interesting about all this is that, although I knew I was in trouble, it was only when I actually realized that I needed help and couldn't carry on that my angel came to me. I didn't cry out for help consciously but I did so unconsciously, and this was enough for my angel.

From now on every day I ask myself two questions. First, 'If someone was watching me now would I be proud of what they saw?' And second, 'If I were to die today, what would I take with me to the afterlife?' If my answer is that I would take shame, fear, guilt, anger, depression or negativity of some kind then I do my best to make changes so that I can make the angels that watch over and guide and protect me proud.

Rachel's story shows that when we discover the inner strength to release negativity, miracles can occur. Isabelle, whose story is below, also experienced the sensation of being watched:

Lighten up

I wasn't fat when I was growing up but I certainly wasn't slender. It wasn't fair because I ate the same amount as my friends but they stayed slim and I got fatter. By the time I was twenty-two I was close to seventeen stone. I pretended to my friends I was happy that way but in secret I would comfort eat. I'd always start the day with good intentions – just a cup of tea and a slice of wholemeal toast – but by coffee time I couldn't resist chocolate or biscuits and once I had succumbed I figured I had nothing to lose so I kept on eating. I only had one meal a day – trouble was, it lasted all day. Somewhere deep down I knew that I needed to change my eating habits but I just didn't know where to start. I was stuck. In many ways my bizarre eating habits shaped and defined my life. There didn't seem to be any way out for me.

Then one night everything changed. It had been a tough day because I'd been at my granddad's funeral. I'm ashamed and honest enough to admit that the contents of the buffet on offer were more on my mind than my granddad was. He'd been ill for a long time so it wasn't like I wasn't expecting him to die, but it was still sad to say goodbye. He'd been a good friend to me when I was a child. I used to see a lot of him. He never used to give me sweets and treats like my nana did but he used to tell me I was beautiful and hearing that often felt as good. But then when I left school he got ill and it was like he didn't recognize me any more.

Anyway, the night after Granddad's funeral I was in the kitchen stalking the contents of the fridge when I had this strange and completely unknown sensation that Granddad was watching me. I can't say why I thought it was him but it just felt like him. Not the him who had been frail and ill but the him I remembered as a child. So, there I was standing by the fridge with a pot of ice cream in my hands and some cheese in another and a bar of chocolate tucked under my arm. I thought about how desperate and ridiculous this must have looked. I can't believe I am saying this but I felt embarrassed. I put the food back in the fridge and sat down.

In the next few days I had this sensation again and again. Every time I made an unnecessary trip to the fridge or was tempted to comfort eat it felt like Granddad was standing behind watching me. It was a huge, and I mean *huge* step for me. It made me realize that food didn't have to control me. I could shut the biscuit tin or the fridge door. Once I was able to flip that mental switch the weight melted away. I'm no twig these days – and I don't want to be – but I'm a healthy weight and feel light not just in body but also in spirit because I know that I'm not alone in all this. Somewhere and somehow someone is watching over me, and making sure I take good care of myself.

My research tells me that a fairly large number of very levelheaded people report this phenomenon of 'someone watching me' or 'someone standing behind me'. Some worry that they might be suffering from some kind of paranoia but I always tell them to relax and trust their instincts if they get this sensation. Once you've made sure that you are not in any actual physical danger – for example, you're not being followed as you walk down the street – just trust that your guardian angel is watching over you and use the sensation to open your heart and ask for guidance and inspiration.

Neither Isabelle nor Rachel were unwell in the physical sense, but they were damaging their health and wellbeing with addictive and out-of-control behaviour. They may have sensed the presence of an angel but the real turning point for both of them was their change of mind.

Poor health can so often be trapped in our bodies and minds

by the way we think and feel about ourselves – once again we return to the theme of low self-esteem and negative thinking limiting the power of the angels to heal us. So if you feel unwell or unhealthy in some way don't add energy to your illness or suffering by dwelling or obsessing about it or thinking there is no way out. There is always a way out, however far away you feel you have strayed. Even when you think it has gone forever, there is always hope.

In much the same way as your thoughts can prolong or create poor health, negative thinking can also trigger premature ageing. As Sonia's story shows, you are only old when you think you are:

Passed me by

It seems like yesterday that I was a teenager but I'm going to celebrate my fiftieth birthday this year. I can't believe I'm going to be almost as old as my mum was when she died aged fifty-one.

When I was growing up I could never imagine myself this age. In my twenties and thirties getting older didn't bother me either. It was when I hit my early forties that I started to worry. The first thing I noticed was this rotten weight gain around my middle and I spent hours at beauty spas and health clubs fighting the flab. I also noticed a big decrease in energy. I really started to need a good night's sleep and if I didn't get it I was absent-minded, forgetful and moody. I read every book I could on anti-ageing and it was a constant topic of conversation with friends. Then to cap it all I was diagnosed with high blood pressure and the menopause really kicked in. My doctor said that if my blood pressure didn't fall within normal limits in six months I would need to get started on medication. And don't get me started on the wrinkles. I spent an awful lot of money on expensive creams that promised to keep my skin looking young and firm but in the end it wasn't creams and lotions that turned back time for me, it was a blind man. Let me explain.

I was out jogging gently one evening when I saw this blind man out walking with his dog on the other side of the road. As I jogged past I could see that he had dropped his scarf and what looked like a wallet but he hadn't noticed. I didn't want to stop my jog because it was part of my fitness plan – and I needed the calorie burn – but I couldn't let this man leave his scarf and wallet behind so I stopped running, crossed the road, picked it up and ran towards him. Just as I was about to reach him he turned around. He must have heard my footsteps and my panting as I was running and he held his stick out defiantly. I realized then how stupid I had been, running up like that to a blind man. He must have thought I was trying to attack him or something. I apologized and told him I was just trying to hand back his scarf and wallet. The man smiled and lowered his stick and I put the scarf in his hand and wallet in his jacket pocket.

While I was doing that the blind man's dog started to lick my hand. The man laughed and it made me laugh too. Then he told me that his dog loved young people and always wanted to lick them. He also told me that he was so happy there were still youngsters like me around willing to lend a helping hand because teenagers were getting such bad press these days. I tried to tell this guy that I was no spring chicken but before I knew it he had turned away with his dog.

You have no idea how amazing it felt to be seen in this way. The simple act of rushing towards this man and lending him a helping hand had transformed me into a young person again in his eyes. As I watched him walk away I got this burst of energy inside me. I sprinted home. Helping out someone less fortunate than myself had made me feel good and feeling good made me feel young and energetic again.

I don't buy expensive creams and potions any more: I donate all that money to good causes. I've cancelled all my gym memberships. I think helping others or thinking about other people rather than yourself is the best anti-ageing product on the market. It gives you such a buzz. My friends want to know my secret to looking young. I tell them the secret is simple: be spontaneous and passionate in your thinking and your actions. Think less about yourself and more about others.

And you know, another great thing happened to me. When I went to the doctor for my check-up my blood pressure was normal again. Sure, I had been careful about my diet and my exercise, but I think the most important factor to change the hardness in my heart was my change of attitude. I don't think about getting older any more and I don't try to hold back the years. I think about living each day to the full so that life and everything that is good about it doesn't pass me by.

In this story change of mind and change of heart seem interchangeable in that this lady's blood pressure lowered when her focus shifted.

The unlocking of some mysterious, miraculous mental-healing potential within each person is known by many people as positive thinking. There is a great deal of research to suggest that the link between health of mind and body is undeniable.

Studies on the placebo effect show that if a person believes they are taking a medicine that will cure them they are more likely to recover, even if that medicine is nothing more than a sugar pill.

The power of positive thinking has been made hugely popular in recent years by brilliant, bestselling books such as *The Secret* by Rhonda Byrne and *You Can Heal Your Life* by Louise Hay. I'm a huge fan of these books and the empowering and positive message they bring. My only concern is that for positive thinking to have true healing power there needs first to be a firm foundation of faith, a belief that extraordinary things can happen. In other words: without faith in the power of love and goodness, positive thinking just doesn't work.

For me, positive thinking without asking the angels for their guidance is reckless because for reasons we may never understand there are some illnesses, misfortunes and suffering in life that no amount of positive thinking can magic away. Sometimes sad and bad things will happen to good people and we feel powerless, lost and alone as a result. Sometimes people fight disease, show remarkable courage and positivity and still die.

It is often said that the greatest lessons in life are learned through pain and suffering; and, while our angels may shed a tear for us, they will not interfere. Sometimes we may be able to look back and understand the reason for it all, or even see that our misfortune was a blessing in disguise, but sometimes, because we are trapped in linear and not spirit time, we may never understand. It is during these difficult, incomprehensible and apparently unjust times when we must face trauma, grief or suffering that it is more important than ever to put our faith and trust in the love, goodness and guidance of our angels, so that if the time comes for us to be called to our spiritual home we can take our guiding angel's hand with loving acceptance, rather than regret.

How to call angels

It is the times when you are sick, feeling lonely or depressed, or lacking energy and unable to motivate yourself, when you most need to call on your angels for their healing support. I'm often asked how to do this and I always reply that there are many ways to do it and no way is right or wrong: you need to find what works best for you.

Some people find that imagining angels placing beams of healing light on their body or simply picturing a radiating light directly to their mind or heart can help, but if this feels a bit strange and odd you can simply talk to your angels, out loud or in your heart. If possible, try to be specific about what you want. You could ask your angels to bring you spiritual healing or to comfort you and give you strength during times of grief or suffering. You could even ask them to guide your doctor or therapist towards the right treatment for you. When asked, angels love to direct you towards the right people, courses, books and teachers to build and enhance your skills or guide you in the right direction.

When you've asked your angels for help, make your mind as receptive as you can so that it is ready to receive guidance and inspiration. This means letting go of negativity, fear and doubt. Picture clearly in your mind the healing that you want in your life or in the lives of others and have unfaltering faith that, with the help of your angels, what you are picturing will come true. Keep repeating your heartfelt desire until it becomes a reality. Trust that, if you persist with faith and do all you can to support your desire, what you create in your mind and your heart your angels will bring to you.

You may also want to ask for healing for someone you know who is sick, someone who is lonely or isolated, someone who is grieving, or for any human need that another person may have. You may even send healing thoughts to someone who is quite well but who you instinctively feel may need a boost of confidence, joy or inspiration. Remember that happy, positive thoughts from one person to another can have a powerful and wonderful effect both on you and the recipient; as we've seen, there is power in prayer.

Perhaps the best way to call on your angels is to acknowledge them as often as you can. Speak to them every day with an open mind and heart – as the vibration of your thoughts, feelings and words can become a clear channel attuned to the angel within you or can set up the right energies for manifesting an angelic encounter in your daily life. Ask your angels to send you a sign and then listen with your spirit and open your heart, not just your eyes and ears.

As you gain experience you'll learn to recognize your own angel signs. For no specific reason you may become aware of the presence of angels in any of the following ways:

- You feel a rush of energy down your spine.
- The air around you starts to tingle and you feel that if you had wings you could fly.
- You feel surrounded by a warm and comforting glow.
- A beautiful aroma (flowers or chocolate are common) may fill the air.
- You may sense that someone is standing behind you but when you turn round there is no one there and you are left with deep feelings of protection and peace.
- You may feel the presence of angelic wings brushing you or wrapping around you.
- You may feel invisible lips kiss your cheek.
- You may hear a voice calling your name – a voice you know is not of this world.
- You may see shafts of coloured lights dancing in front of you.
- You may notice a gentle ringing in your ear – not the high-pitched tone of tinnitus, just a gentle hum for a few seconds.
- You may notice an increase in coincidences that occur in your life or that problems solve themselves in unexpected ways.
- Your dreams may become more vivid.
- If you ask your angel for a sign they may manifest in the unexplained appearance of white feathers. You may also notice unusual cloud formations or flowers that last for longer than usual or hear the word 'angel' in a song or on the radio or in the most unlikely context.

These are just some of the infinite number of angel signs you may see or notice after you have called on your angels. When you do notice them, just relax and enjoy the sensation of being watched over and cared for. The truth is that angelic signs can be found everywhere, if you look at the world through the eyes of your inner angel; and, the more you see angels in everyone and everything, the more you become like them and the more alive you feel because you are bringing heaven down to earth.

In my work I often find myself referencing William Blake, the English poet who saw angels all his life, because he once said that he could see 'a world in a grain of sand' and 'a heaven in a wildflower'. So why not 'hold infinity in the palm of your hand' and see an angel in a grain of sand, a wildflower, a bird, a white feather, a cloud, a sunrise, a smile, a song, a hug or anything else that inspires you or speaks to your heart?

The more conscious you are of miracles the more likely they are to manifest around you, so why not let an angel heal your body, mind and spirit through your dreams, your conscience, the magic of coincidence and answered prayers or through the voices of those you love.

Why not let this book work a miracle of healing inside you by helping you to see the universe for what it truly is: a place of unexpected wonder where people can survive against all odds, where miracle healing can occur, where grief and fear can be replaced by comfort and love and where angels can walk among us.

Heavenward

In order to catch a star you must open your heart. You must look at it, contemplating with admiration, feeling affection and genuine tenderness. Then, close your eyes, be still for a moment, look again at your heart. You'll find that wonderful light living in you now.

Author unknown

Hopefully reading the true stories in this book will have opened your eyes to the very real possibility that angels exist. I hope it will have also opened your eyes to the possibility that you don't always need overt signs or messages from them in order to believe that they are here to watch over you. Your life has already been touched by an angel in a myriad number of ways but you just haven't realized it. Reflect on your life and see if the healing power of angels is already there, just waiting for you to recognize and embrace it.

Angels are there whether you believe in them or not, but the more you believe in them the more likely you are to recognize them when you meet them. I hope and trust that the next time angels cross your path – and they will cross your path – you will see them.

Never forget how much your angels love you and how much they want you to live in health and happiness. Just ask for their guidance and then look within you and around you for the divine answers they will give to your questions. And the more you listen and look for your angels the more you will find yourself soaring heavenward, because angels will always guide you towards your real self – to the divine part of you where there is no fear, pain or sickness; only laughter, love and goodness. You may not always be able to stay on the true path of goodness but, however far you may stray into darkness, it is that spark of goodness with which you were born that the angels can always see within you and which will always lead you back into their light.

Above all, remember that angels prove that impossible things really can and do happen. That life is a miracle and that each one of us is a miracle. So, if your life today is not as healthy, fulfilling or happy as it could and should be, I hope and trust that reading this book has shown you that you are not alone and that with the help of your angels you can move from suffering to healing and from fear to love. By tuning into their divine messages you have all you need to create a wonderful and healthy life for yourself – a life that doesn't end with death; a life where miracles are only a thought and an open heart away.

I shall leave you, for now, with one of my favourite angel blessings and before that some angelic words to ponder:

A pearl is a beautiful thing that is produced by an injured life. It is the tear from the injury of the oyster. The treasure of our being in this world is also produced by an injured life. If we had not been wounded, if we had not been injured, then we will not produce the pearl.

Stephan Hoeller

Angel blessing

Angels around us, angels beside us, angels within us. Angels are watching over you when times are good or stressed. Their wings wrap gently around you, whispering you are loved and blessed.

About the Author

Theresa Cheung was born into a family of psychics and spiritualists. Since gaining a Masters from King's College, Cambridge she has been involved in the study of the psychic world for more than twenty-five years. She is the author of a variety of books, including the international bestsellers *The Element Encyclopaedia of 20,000 Dreams* and *The Element Encyclopaedia of the Psychic World* and the *Sunday Times* bestsellers *An Angel Called My Name*, *An Angel on My Shoulder* and *Angel Babies*. Her books have been translated into twenty-five different languages and her writing has featured in *It's Fate*, *Spirit and Destiny* and *Prediction* magazines. She has also worked on books for Derek Acorah, Yvette Fielding and Tony Stockwell.

Theresa believes that this book was born in answer to her own questions and as a gift for herself and others. She has a strong interest in angels, spirit guides, dreams and visions of the afterlife and feels that angels are directing her writing and her life. She has also had a number of angel encounters herself, some of which she shares here.

Calling all angels

If you have had an angel experience and wish to share it with Theresa, she would love to hear from you. Please contact her care of Simon and Schuster, 1st Floor, 222 Gray's Inn Road, London WC1X 8HB or email any inspiring and uplifting stories direct to her at: angeltalk710@aol.com